CW01083872

Beef, Bacon and Bag Pudding

Old Berkshire in the Civil War

by

David Disbury.

About the author

David Disbury was born in Surrey. Trained as a chef, after national service he began a career with the post office, retiring as a Training and Development Manager with the Royal Mail.

Studying archaeology, local history and genealogy he has gained a university extra-mural diploma and qualification in these subjects.

With a lifelong interest in the history of Berkshire, the Vale of the White Horse in particular, he has written a number of books and articles on the areas archaeological and local history.

With ancestors in the Vale going back over three hundred years, one of whom rode with Sir Robert Pye's Troop of Horse, he now devotes his time to the study and teaching of genealogy and family history.

First published by
Timescape Publishing
The Thatched Cottage
Manor Farm
Kerdiston
Reepham
Norfolk
NR10 4RY

TIMESCAPE.CO.UK

© Timescape Publishing\ D.G. Disbury

All rights reserved. Apart from fair dealing for the purpose of study, research, criticism or review, as permitted under the Copyright Designs and Patents Act, 1988, no part of this publication may be reproduced, stored in a retrieval system, or transmitted in any form or by any means, electronic, electrical, chemical, mechanical, photocopying, recording or otherwise, without the prior permission of the copyright owner. Enquiries should be addressed to the publishers.

ISBN 0 9531851 1 7

Typeset in Worcester 12pt solid

Produced and printed in England by
Albion Graphics, Norfolk.

CONTENTS

PREFACE

This volume first came to my attention some years ago having appeared in several bibliographies in more general books on the English Civil War. My initial attempts to track down an original copy were fruitless and it was only by chance that I came across a copy in a second hand bookshop in Norfolk. After reading the text I was amazed that no one had thought to reprint such a well researched work. Several phone calls later I managed to contact the author, David Disbury, and we quickly reached an agreement.

David informed me that he had originally privately produced only 200 copies and although approached by several publishers nothing more had come of it. I was happy to remedy this oversight.

The text has been left much as it was when first published 20 years ago. A little judicious editing has taken place and a new section has been added by way of an appendix but otherwise the main body of the book is as David originally wrote it.

It may, of course, be said that certain sections of the original text are now a little outdated, having been superceded by more recent research, but taken as a whole it remains a classic study of the English Civil War. Although now over 20 years since it was written this book has stood the test of time and has much to offer anyone with an interest in Englands past.

Timescape. May 1998

INTRODUCTION

(To the original edition)

This book is an attempt to relate the story of one county and its people during the Great Civil War. Famous battles and sieges have not been overlooked but these have been seen through the eyes of the soldier and villager, not the eyes of the historian or politician. I have tried to remove the false glamour of the Cavalier and Roundhead and replace it with the reality of civil war.

No book on Berkshire dealing with this period in English history could be written without acknowledgement to the monumental research undertaken by Walter Money. The Thomason Tracts are quoted by permission of the British Library. I would like to thank the staff of the Egham and Reading Libraries for their tireless assistance, Margaret Clark for reading the manuscript and for making so many helpful suggestions, Patricia Tipper for typing the finished copy, and last but not least, my wife who, with few complaints, endured many years of the Civil War long after it was fought.

D. G. Disbury. Egham 1978.

CHAPTER ONE

BERKSHIRE 1625-1642

'There is no astrologer, then say I,
Can search more deep in this than I,
To give you a reason from the stars
What causeth peace or Civil Wars.'
Martin Parker, 1642 (1)

Where 17th century astrologers failed, modern historians have succeeded in suggesting a multitude of causes for the start of the English Civil War. Among the many factors that led to the final decline into bloodshed are listed the unbending character of King Charles, the rise of a new wealthy middle class and even a latent Marxism in the lower classes. Although all these factors must surely have played their part it must be understood that the true causes of the war lay somewhere among the complex financial, religious and political issues that stretched back over three reigns. Most of the causes are mirrored in the county of Berkshire during the first 17 years of the reign of Charles the first.

Thomas Fuller, in his 'Worthies of England', described 17th century Berkshire 'as plentiful as any county in England of the common commodities, grass, grain, fish, fowl, wool and wood etc'. Fuller never wrote a truer word. The Berkshire that he knew was indeed a rich county, one of the richest in the whole Kingdom. Trout were taken from the river Kennet at Hungerford and eels from the Thames at Abingdon. Wool from the downland sheep made its way to the great cloth making centres of Newbury and Reading. The great woodlands gave supplies of fine timber that were transported by barge to markets as far afield as London and the continent. The county grew rich on profits from farming and the wool industry.

This industry was enhanced by the naturally good trade routes that crossed the county. The great western highway, linking the rich produce lands of the west country with London, passed through the area bringing in its wake profits and trade for towns such as Newbury, Reading and Hungerford. Faringdon and Abingdon both prospered from the traffic that flowed along the major roads that they stood astride and the traffic along the Thames made cheap transport of vast quantities of goods an attractive option. A county as well supplied with goods and transport as Berkshire was at the beginning of the 17th century was the perfect base for the operations of the wealthy rising merchant class.

This new merchant class had, in effect, replaced much of the old nobility of England. They built a new aristocracy based upon trade and business and with their rise came the emergence of new ideas. When Charles the first came to the throne in 1625 he found himself master of a country that was looking to the future while his own administration was still based on a long outdated Elizabethan system. The merchants wanted reform. Charles wanted control.

Within three months of his accession Charles arrived at Windsor. It was claimed that the court brought with them plague and popery, they certainly brought money troubles. 'They are in such straights for money at court as is not to be spoken,' records the state papers.(2)

Financial problems dominated Charles' reign. Due to inflation and other factors the fixed income of the Royal Household was no longer enough to cover the costs of Charles' court. To raise taxes needed the approval of Parliament but Charles realised after early unsuccessful attempts that Parliament was only willing to grant money in exchange for reforms. This the King was unwilling to do. He believed that as monarch he was, appointed directly by God and had to answer to no other than the almighty himself. Charles' answer was to attempt to rule without the aid of Parliament.

This art of personal rule had been perfected by his father, James I, and the old Queen Elizabeth and as long as there was no major expense to be covered, Charles could continue for many years without calling a new Parliament. Money was available in small quantities and by manipulating existing methods of money collection this could be increased. Unfortunately, Charles' methods, already considered dubious by many of his subjects, were taken to extremes. Forced and voluntary loans were raised on entire towns, inheritances confiscated from minors and fees were charged for accepting a knighthood, fines for refusing. What finally brought matters to a head was the raising of the hated 'Ship money'.

'Ship money' was a tax originally levied only on coastal towns and communities in times of national threat to help pay for the navy. Charles reasoned that if the coastline was threatened then the inland areas could also be considered under threat and widened the tax to cover all communities. He also declared that as the navy was now a full time concern then the tax should be raised annually to cover its costs. Far more money was of course raised than was spent on the navy and the merchants, all being good book keepers, realised they were being exploited. It was all very well for the monarch to reject their reforms, that they could live with, but to attack their wallets was quite a different matter. Charles started to meet pockets of organised resistance.

Charles' alienation of the merchant classes was further heightened by what the puritan elements of the population saw as his leanings towards the Catholic church, or popery, as it was called. His marriage to the Catholic Henrietta Maria had brought a large retinue of priests to England and their celebrating Mass at Whitehall and continued contact with Rome only added fuel to the puritans flames. Both puritan and Protestant alike felt that they were being betrayed by their own monarch.

All the real and imagined fears of the period are reflected in the town and county records of Berkshire. Reading, the then county town, was an important political and trade centre. Placed, as it was, astride the Bath road and a mere 40 miles from London it boasted a population of nearly 5000, large by the standards of the day, and held the rights to a market, a weekly court and its own prison. The town housed substantial Royal stables and its main industries consisted of brewing, saltpetre production (an ingredient of gunpowder) but primarily, the cloth trade. The town could boast of its fine woolens and a large part of the population relied upon this

Great Seal of Charles the first.

single industry for employment.

Charles' habit of becoming embroiled in foreign wars was, of course, harmful to the cloth trade of Berkshire. Restraints were placed upon exports to the traditional customers in places such as Delft and Emden and in 1630 the towns merchants felt obliged to complain of the loss of trade they had suffered in 'mingled and coloured cloths'. (4) Two years later they again complained that where formerly 150 cloths were produced weekly demand had now dropped to 40 or even less. The Counties 'formerly good clothing towns are now decayed', they claimed.

Reading was not alone in its suffering. Newbury, the sister clothing town, faced similar problems and the town leaders constantly battled against rising unemployment and the increased cost of poor relief. So desperate did the situation become that the town council instructed the ale house keepers to stop selling beer in the hope that it would deter the groups of disgruntled unemployed from gathering in such places. Reading followed Newbury's lead and forbade the sale of beer to inn keepers only further adding to the unemployment. Workhouses purchased machines to manufacture cloth and then lost money producing goods that would not sell.

For the poor people of Berkshire things went from bad to worse. An increase in demand for food from the rapidly growing city of London sent local corn prices soaring. Justices of the peace tried to keep Reading market prices down for fear of not being able to feed their own townsfolk (6) but with limited effect and for many starvation became a reality.

The desperation of the locals drove them to wild acts and in one case a convoy of food carts was attacked by women and children on the Newbury to Reading road. Newbury magistrates sentenced the women to be whipped for their insolence in not wanting to starve. (7) Guards were placed on further carts and the assembly of groups of men and women were forbidden.

The people of Berkshire suffered much in the early 1630's and felt that they had been badly treated by the Royal government. Idle hands and empty bellies made them all the more belligerent and it did not take a great orator to stir their feelings up into actions and it was not long before the rising puritan movement took advantage of this fact.

The puritans had their very own axe to grind in connection with the monarchy. Charles had appointed William Laud, the son of a Reading clothier, to the post of Archbishop of Canterbury (8). Lauds ancestry was in his favour as far as Berkshire was concerned but his views were definitely held against him by the puritan sects in the the county. His leanings towards the so called 'Arminians' and the high church establishment put him directly at odds with the puritan movement and his encouragement of the return to vestments, ritual and altars smacked of popery. To the puritans the smell of incense was closely linked with the smell of brimstone and burning Protestant martyrs.

It was not very long before the puritans were given new martyrs. Odowick Bowyer slandered Laud and was sentenced to stand in the pillory in London. His punishment included his being brought to Reading and there to be nailed by his ears to the pillory. He was branded on the face, fined and imprisoned for life.(9) Actions such as these led to just as strong a reaction.

Puritan vicars began preaching against the Arminians and included politics in their sermons. Edward Rood, vicar of St. Helens, Abingdon, was reported for his 'preaching to adventure on state business, and among the rest has denied the King's supremacy'. The state began to clamp down hard upon the transgressors and no offence was too small for the attention of the Star chamber. Windsor singers had already been warned over there singing of 'lewd songs'. (10)

By the mid 1630's the feeling of the population had turned against the King. They were unhappy, felt that they had been treated badly, exploited for money and generally held to be of little account. They were unhappy but they were not yet ready to turn in anger and violence against their true and appointed monarch. This would only happen later and was really only made possible by some stunningly insensitive actions on the part of Charles himself.

By 1636 there were two main talking points in Reading, plague and ship money. Thirteen people had died and a number of town houses had been shut up in the latest epidemic. The town leaders were hard pressed to control the anxiety and worry of the population and the new row that arose over the assessment of the ship money only added to their burden. At an assessment meeting, held in a local court, Sir Francis Knollys argued that, from his experience of ships and the county rates, the money paid in the previous year was more than sufficient to cover this year as well. Following up his outburst by storming from the meeting Knollys was found to be 'in contempt' and was made to apologize to the Sheriff of Berkshire. Notwithstanding Knollys' objections that year Berkshire was assessed to raise £4000, Windsor £100, Wokingham £50, Reading £220, Newbury £120, Abingdon £100, Wallingford £20, and the Dean and Chapter of Windsor £30. (11)

Sir Francis Knollys' objections to the assessment were not merely on grounds of principle. He obviously realised that the once rich county of Berkshire was in desperate financial trouble. In January 1637 the council of state admonished the Mayor of Newbury over his failure to collect and pay the levy. Henry Rawson of Windsor was sent to prison for the same offence. In May, John Hawthorne, on behalf of the sheriff was in a position to pay £3600 for the county. It took until September to obtain the remainder.

Ship money affected everybody, rich and poor alike, directly and indirectly. Calls were made for a new Parliament to be raised before Ship money, or any other form of taxation, was levied and John Hampden, a Buckinghamshire landowner, started a test case against ship money calling it an illegal tax.

The Hampden case was a turning point in the reign of Charles I. A year later the judges returned a split verdict in the King's favour but the very fact that judges appointed by, and paid by, the King had found against him showed the extent of the peoples resentment. The general population saw Hampden as the moral victor and a small shockwave shuddered through the court. Charles chose to ignore it.

If the King's court advisors saw the danger in the verdict given in the Hampden trial they completely failed to see the danger of a war with Scotland.

Archbishop Laud and the church authorities had drawn up a new church liturgy for use in Scotland based upon the English practice and attempted to force its introduction. The powerful Scottish Kirk rejected what it saw as English interference and in a typical overreaction abolished episcopacy altogether. This was more than the King could stomach. For half his realm to place themselves above his rule and ignore Royal commands was seen by the King as an act of rebellion,

Charles, overreacting to the Scottish overreaction, attempted to bring his wayward subjects to heel by force. An ill prepared and ill equipped army was sent north and a military disaster followed shortly afterwards.

Charles failed to realise that the problems he faced in England were almost as severe as those he faced in Scotland. Puritan preachers, strongly supportive of the Scots stance openly preached against the war. One Newbury preacher going as far as commending 'the Scots in points of religion, fasting and prayer etc.'. He went on to warn the soldiers to 'arm themselves with the armour of his text'. Ephes. V1.12

General discontent and the support of the Puritans meant that it became increasingly difficult for the King to raise the troops for his war in Scotland. Men pressed for service in Berkshire mutinied at Daventry, in Northamptonshire and 'withdrew themselves from the Kings service without licence, and returned back into the counties where they had been pressed'. The attitude to the Second Bishops War was, if anything, worse. Soldiers pressed in Berkshire ran as far away as Somerset and press men in the Vale of the White horse had difficulty in even finding able bodied men as they were hidden by 'their families and landowners alike'.

Captain William Lower, escorting men from Reading, was threatened with having his brains beaten out by men convinced 'that they were to be shipped and sold for slaves, that the officers had false commissions, that the King gave them no authority, that they would be used like dogs, that all was peace in Scotland, and it was only a pretence to carry them elsewhere, that all and my Lord General himself were Papists'. It is not difficult to see the hand of the puritan preachers in such allegations as these.

War with Scotland really signalled the beginning of the end for Charles I. Had he found a peaceful way of settling the dispute then it is likely that he could have survived indefinitely without the need to call Parliament. Revenues, no matter how unpopular their method of raising, were just about sufficient for his needs. But war cost money and to raise sufficient taxes left the King with no alternative but to call a Parliament. On the advice of his most loyal advisor, Thomas Wentworth, Charles called a Parliament for the spring of 1640.

In the countryside the court agents were already feeling out any areas of likely opposition and assessing the amount of support that they were likely to receive. In Berkshire Sir Samuel Sawyer reported back to Windebank's secretary on local views and he stated that he hoped to secure the votes of Lord Craven's tenants in the Vale of the White Horse, Alderman Pratt's at Coleshill and Lady Banbury's at Cholsey. It would be done he said 'either from fear or love'. He continued, 'Sir Robert Pye may do his lordship some service with those about Faringdon'.

Election fever gripped the county and George Purefoy, Sheriff of Berkshire, complained that hopes of an election and a Parliament made the collection of ship money impossible. 'Truly sir, to deal plainly with you I conceive the main ground of the slackness..... is the expectation that they have of a Parliament that it will be represented to the King as a grievance, whereby they hope to obtain remission thereof'.

Three candidates stood for Abingdon, Sir George Stonehouse, Bulstrode Whitelock and Sir Robert Knollys. Later Knollys withdrew as candidate and left Stonehouse, a court sympathiser, to win the seat. Whitelock, disappointed by his defeat, peevishly wrote, 'He persuaded by his beef, bacon and bag-pudding, and by permitting as many as would be drunk at his charge, at the alehouse in the town.' (21)

This 'Short lived' Parliament, as the Parliament of 1640 became known, was filled with members who were intransigent to the King's demands and were ready only to air the grievances that they had been harbouring for so many years. After three fruitless months, at least as far as the King was concerned, Parliament was dissolved.

Anxious to reassure the population as a whole that even without a Parliament their voice would be heard, Charles requested that the county representatives deal directly with him. Grand juries were not slow to do so and the jury serving the assizes for Berkshire delivered its petition on the 11 July 1640. The rather wordy petition outlined all the pent up frustrations felt within the county at the time.

Top of the petition was, of course, the ever hated ship money. Berkshire could not, and would not, pay the latest demands. New taxes had been introduced on top of the old compelling freemen to 'hiding themselves in woods'. The county was being denude of labour, the harvest was being left in the fields and families were having to be supported by the parish funds which daily grew smaller. (23)

One particular Berkshire grievance concerned what was known as 'forest law'. 'Your majesties forests of Windsor are particularly burdened with the innumerable increase in deer, which if they shall go on as fast... will leave neither food or room for any other creature in the forest'. The killing of the Kings deer was a major offence and the strictly enforced laws were exacerbated by the increasing enclosure of land to feed the Royal herds. Local feeling was so strong that it finally spilled over into violence.

Attempts by the authorities to arrest those responsible for breaking the forest law merely made matters worse and in September 1642 a large crowd invaded the park armed with guns. Over 200 deer were killed and fences thrown down and the disturbances continued into the following year. The government attitude hardened and rioters were even sent to Newgate but still the so called 'riots in the park' continued. (24)

Undeterred by the Parliaments refusal to grant him money, the King embarked on the 'Second Bishops War' with Scotland. This was, if anything, even more disastrous than the first and was marked by military defeat, mutinies in the army and ended with a Scottish army occupying the north of England. Charles' loss of face was only outdone by his loss of money as the Scots army demanded a daily payment to the tune of £850. This amount to be payable until a permanent treaty had been ratified. Charles was left with no alternative but to call another Parliament.

The Scottish armies presence in England, loss of trade, unemployment and yet another outbreak of plague, was the background to the election campaign. Considering the issues the county elections were fairly uneventful and the same candidates were returned as before. Known to history as the 'Long Parliament' it was the last to be called by Charles Stuart, King of England.

Relentlessly the Court party was hounded at Westminster. Thomas Wentworth, now Earl of Strafford, was tried and condemned to death by a Bill of Attainder. Mr William Taylor, burgess of Windsor was expelled from the hostile Commons for daring to speak against Strafford's attainder, describing it as to 'commit murder with the Sword of Justice'. (25) Archbishop Laud was placed in the Tower and on 12 May 1641 he heard that Wentworth had been executed. The Bill of Attainder needed the Royal signature and this, albeit reluctantly, the King gave. For this, Laud wrote of Charles, he 'knew not how to be or be made great'.

The same day he had agreed the bill of attainder, Charles assented to Parliament being called in future every three years and the present Parliament remaining until it chose to dissolve itself. Pym went from strength to strength, ruthlessly the authority vested in the King was being transferred to Parliament. When it came to the control of the armed forces the King made a stand. Fearing also a bill being introduced against his Queen he attempted a coup d'etat. In January 1642, the King led armed men into the House with the aim of arresting five of his leading critics. He failed on two levels, one, the birds had flown and two, any doubts held by moderates were hardened against him. Both Houses united in condemnation of the Royal move against Westminster. Six days after the abortive coup the King left London. It was the last time he would see the capital as a free man.

Charles reached Windsor on January 12 and it was not long before a Parliament spy, Mr Bagshaw of the town, reported the King was recruiting and arming an army. 400 horse rode into the castle and messengers were sent up and down the country to Royalist sympathizers. (26) Pym used the information to foment more opposition in Parliament. In February Charles escorted his Queen to the coast where she embarked for Holland. Her mission was to sell the Royal jewels to buy arms and ammunition; England was close to Civil War.

Support for Parliament came from all over the country. On 5 March 1642 Berkshire presented its petition to Westminster.

'To the Right Honourable the Lords now assembled in Parliament. The humble Petition of the High-Sheriff, Knights, Esquiors, Gentlemen, Ministers, Freeholders, and other inhabitants of the County of Berks. Sheweth, That your Petitioners with all joy and thankfullness of heart, acknowledge the happy concurrence of your Lordships, with the honourable House of Commons, to the affecting of many great and excellent things. And we hope of a full and perfect Reformation in the Government of this Church and Commonwealth ..... earnestly desiring your Lordships assistance, in putting our Countie, together with all other Counties of this Kingdom into a present Posture of Defence, and we shall be ever ready with our Lives, Powers and Fortunes, to maintain and defend His Majesties Person, Honour and Estate, your Lordships in that happy concurrence, and the Rights and Privileges of Parliament.' (27)

Over the next unhappy years many lives, powers and fortunes would be lost and the inhabitants of Berkshire would be petitioning for an accommodation between King and Parliament to end the terrible war.

CHAPTER TWO

CIVIL WAR ARMIES

'Let me speak proudly: tell the Constable
We are but warriors for the working-day;'
Henry V

The Pressed Men

Prior to the Civil War England had no standing army. For military service abroad the government would resort to a 'press'. The prison and the alehouse supplied the needs of the army. During the King's foreign wars Berkshire's reaction to the press typified the country as a whole. In 1627 of the 50 men levied in the county for the expedition to La Rochelle, 32 arrived at Plymouth with their (1) conductor. The First Bishops War with Scotland resulted in a press in 1639. The Berkshire and Oxfordshire men were conducted north but on reaching Daventry 'withdrew themselves from the King's service, without licence, and returned back into the counties where they had been pressed'. (2) Parts of the county were slower to provide their quota of soldiers than others, the Vale of the White Horse being particularly reluctant to comply. Deputy Lieutenant George Stonehouse of Radley, writing in July 1640, complained, 'only 120 coated, others ran away after they were enlisted in the Vale division.' (3) Sir Edmund Sawyer compiled notes for the King's secretary on the difficulty of pressing men in Berkshire. 'Divers men fittest to serve, where they hear of the press, run away and hide in the woods and other places, and are cherished by their parents or masters until the press is passed.' Thomas Goldsmith of Maidenhead along with John Winch and John Peveral of Bray, were committed to prison for refusing press money, they all later escaped from prison. One pressed man came before the High Constable of Bray. On being beaten by his officer he had drawn his sword and threatened to kill him, the constables sent the soldier to prison for a week.

One of the worst violent incidents concerning pressed men and their officers happened at Faringdon in June 1640. A large party of Dorset pressed men were being conducted north and they billeted at Faringdon overnight. Lieutenant William Mohun, on being defied and threatened with a drum-stick, struck the offending drummer's hand off with his sword. Word passed among the soldiers that the drummer had died and they mustered into troops and marched into Faringdon High Street. They discovered Mohun in company with a captain and ensign. The three officers, in fear of their lives, retreated into an inn. Chased up the stairs and into a bedchamber they tried to escape by climbing out of the window and along the pole that carried the inn-sign. The soldiers below began throwing stones to dislodge the officers and the captain and ensign climbed back through the window. Mohun still clung on with the stones whistling all round him. One enterprising soldier fetched an eighteen foot long pike and managed to poke the officer until he fell into the street. The mob beat him half to death and dragging him by the hair tried to finish him by drowning in the open sewer. Thinking him dead they continued to drag the body about the town, finally throwing him in a ditch. A small boy later saw Mohun crawl from the ditch into a nearby house and reported this to the soldiers. They returned to their victim and dashed out his brains with clubs and hung his remains in the pillory. The whole force made off into Wiltshire leaving the officers to bury the lieutenant in Faringdon churchyard. A hue and cry was set up using militia from Berkshire and eventually five Dorsetmen were hanged at Abingdon for the murder. (4) Pressing was obviously not popular.

The Trained Bands

For the defence of the Kingdom the reigning monarch had at his or her calling, the Trained Bands. Local militia were provided by a system that required estate and land holders to supply, at their expense, given numbers of horsemen. Males over the age of sixteen could be called as foot soldiers. The term 'Trained' was rather loose, it meant that each county could muster into bands groups of men for training, not that they had ready trained units. Over one hundred years of peace within the realm resulted in the 'able' men envisioned by Queen Elizabeth, being ready only 'to give their captain a brave volley of shot at his entrance into his inn'. (5) Early in his reign Charles had to reprove, through his Privy Council, the lord lieutenants of the counties over their neglect of the Trained Bands. In 1626 Viscount Wallingford reported that in the event of an emergency Berkshire had 'but 1000 armed men in the whole county.' (6) The Royal admonishment only resulted in a return in 1629 of 1000 foot, 80 horse and small supplies of ammunition at Abingdon and Reading, for use in Berkshire. The deputy lieutenants were constantly certifying the names of men who either failed to attend musters or when doing so were defective in arms. Andrew Boreman of Reading was reported for refusing to pay the muster masters in April 1632 and 'Examples such as this led others not to attend the musters'. The deputy lieutenant for the Forest Division returned the names of 14 persons either being defective in arms or refusing to attend for training in September 1638.

The attitude of Berkshire's men to the soldierly arts was typical of most. The London Trained Bands are one exception as some of their companies did train and drill, their record during the war was to reflect this. Berkshire retained this apathy throughout the war. But then the county-men did not share the luxury of the agricultural labourer who, when told of the battle at Marston Moor, expressed surprise that King and Parliament 'had fallen out'. The constant movement of armies across Berkshire, the starvation and hardship of Civil War, made them fully aware. No famous regiment emerged from the county. Perhaps a John Hampden would have altered this, some Berkshire men did serve, with distinction, in his famous Greencoat Regiment.

Cavaliers and Roundheads
Both terms were first used as insults. The first reflected what was considered the attitude of the Royalists and the second the manner of hair cut worn by London apprentices who rapidly joined the Parliament army.

Principally the Civil War armies came from three sources. The cavalry, or 'Horse', was made up of gentlemen volunteers. The infantry, or 'Foot', were enlisted from the plentiful unemployed of London and East Anglia; lastly there were the pressed men. Both sides welcomed any professional soldier with experience from the continental wars. Much of the officer class was made up of these soldiers,

15

A true and exact Relation of the
manner of his Maiesties setting up of His
Standard at *Nottingham*, on Munday the
22. of August 1642.

First, The forme of the Standard, as it is here figured, and who were present at the advancing of it

Secondly, The danger of setting up of former Standards, and the damage
which ensued thereon.

Thirdly, A relation of all the Standards that ever were set up by any King.

Fourthly, the names of those Knights who are appointed to be the Kings
Standard-bearers. With the forces that are appoynted to guard it.

Fifthly, The manner of the Kings comming first to *Coventry*.

Sixtly, The *Cavalieres* resolution and dangerous threats which they have
uttered, if the King concludes a peace without them, or hearkens unto
his great Councell the Parliament : Moreover how they have shared
and divided *London* amongst themselves already.

A contemporary pamphlet depicting the raising of the King's
standard.

the two most famous being Prince Rupert and Sir William Waller. Yet, like so many wars England has faced, completely unprepared, farmers, merchants and tradesmen, became brilliant soldiers. Men without previous experience became great captains, John Hampden from Buckinghamshire, Robert Pye from Berkshire and most famous of all, Oliver Cromwell from Huntingdonshire. The Royalists had the noblemen's sons, practiced in the arts of war or skilful in the saddle. The Parliamentarians had men like Captain Margery of Pye's regiment of whom Cromwell wrote, 'I had rather have a plain russet coated captain that knows what he fights for, and loves what he knows, than that which you call gentleman and is nothing (7) else'.

The Horse

Ideally a cavalry regiment would consist of 420 officers and men, divided into six troops. The regiment took its name from its colonel. Prior to the formation of the New Model Army, most regiments were undermanned, apart from Cromwell's. Regiments were made up of as many troops as the colonel could manage to raise with between 50 and 70 men per troop. Each troop would have a captain, lieutenant, cornet, quartermaster, 3 corporals, 2 trumpeters, a farrier, a saddler and, hopefully, 60 troopers. Contrary to popular belief Royalist and Parliamentarian looked very much alike in dress. They wore 'lobster- tailed' helmets, metal 'pots' or the soft felt hats of the period. A leather buff-coat with deep skirts and a breast and backplate protected the body. They were armed with pistols and swords although carbines used early in the war were later confined to officers.

The cornet carried the troop colour. Each had a design and motto, usually religious in content but not always. Captain Brown's troop colour had a skull and laurel wreath with the motto 'One of these', and a Royalist captain had a picture of a trooper holding a sword in one hand and something less war-like in the other. The motto, in Latin, meant 'Ready with either weapon.'

Dragoons

Dragoons were little more than mounted

infantry. Their mounts were nags, far inferior to cavalry horses. Trained to fight from the saddle it was more usual for them to dismount and fight while one in ten held the animals. Dragoons fought in loose formations or secured bridges and roads, they were armed with firelocks, a forerunner of the flintlock, or fowling pieces.

The Foot

Infantry consisted of two types, pikemen and musketeers. The pike was eighteen feet long, made of ash wood and topped with two feet of steel. The men lined up in files of six-deep and when charged by cavalry would lower the pike, resting it against the instep. At 'push of pike' it would be wielded point and butt against other foot soldiers. Considered to be the 'more honourable' weapon it required a strong man to use it. At Newbury it was the pikemen that held back Rupert's cavalry. Firepower had failed to halt his charge but he made 'no impression on their stand of pikes'. In the same battle John Gwyn recorded 'a whole file of men, six deep, with their heads all struck off by one cannon shot of ours.. '. For protection the pikemen wore a corselet of back and breast, a helmet with flaps protected their heads.

Musketeers should have numbered two to every one pikeman, a number rarely achieved. When attacked the musketeers would interline with the pikes, if the attack was from cavalry they would form a great circle called a 'hedgehog' from the bristling pikes. The musket was a heavy matchlock requiring a rest to fire from. The match was called a serpent and it wound round the arm and butt of the weapon. The match had to be alight all the time in action, making it dangerous near powder and a giveaway at night. Powder was contained in twelve wooden containers known as 'apostles'. Bullets were carried in a shoulder bag and one in the mouth in action. Pikemen and musketeers carried cheap swords.

Identification

There was little to tell a Cavalier from a Roundhead. Each side adopted the wearing of sashes or scarves about their waists. Royalists favoured red and Parliament, orange-tawny. Prior to an engagement some other identification would be given. At Newbury the Earl of Essex had his men wear a green bough in their hats. Call signs or passwords were used, at the relief of

Basing Colonel Gage used the password 'St George.'

Clothing

There was certainly a lot of uniformity in regimental wear.
Colonels coated their men according to whim or what they could
afford. A Parliament contract specified that breeches should be
made from 'Reading cloth'. Once made, the trousers, with linings,
were shrunk in cold water before issue.

Colours

The colour and insignia of the regiments were strictly laid down.
The colonels colour was plain. The lieutenant-colonel's plain
with a St George's cross in the top corner next to the staff. The
descending order of rank from major to sixth captain had devices
wrought on the colour. Each standard was 6 feet square.

The Artillery

The Artillery Train was made up of various sized guns. The field
guns were called sakers, minions and falcons. The larger cannon
were cannon-royale and demi-cannon, these along with mortars
were reserved for siege warfare. Apart from the ever-present fear of
bursting barrels, there was the fear of a spark firing powder kegs.
At the siege of Reading 'giving fire to a peece, by chance fired the
barrels, and blew up the carriage, and killed 3 or 4 men outright.'
(8) At the first battle of Newbury the King set his cannon on Wash
Common (near the present Gun public house). The Roundheads
had theirs sited on Round Hill and one of the only artillery duels
of the war was fought out. Cannon filled with case-shot could
wreak terrible havoc among the closely packed foot. At Newbury
Sergeant Foster described it as 'somewhat dreadful when bowels
and brains flew in our faces.' So much for the glamour of
Cavaliers and Roundheads.

Religion

A lot of the Parliament propaganda was
directed at the high proportion of 'Papists' in
the King's army. It is true that a number of
Catholic soldiers served the King and it was
certain that there were no Catholics fighting
for Parliament. Apart from their spiritual
guidance, chaplains served another useful

19

function. Firth called them the first war correspondents and a number of tracts recording battles certainly bears this out. Manchester's chaplain, Simeon Ashe, was the author of 'A True Relation of the late Occurences at and since the late Battle of Newbury.' (9)

When army power was at its height and the Army Grandees were 'celebrating' Christmas at Windsor, they were visited by Mr Saltmarsh, a chaplain. Saltmarsh enjoyed 'revelations' and he informed the officers that God was 'highly displeased' with them over their treatment of the 'Saints' serving God in the army. Later his tract was titled '.... giving seasonable advice to the Lord General, Lieutenant-General, and the Council of War'.

Pay

Normally pay was something a Civil War soldier received if he was very lucky. Many times colonels paid from their own purse to prevent mutiny or desertion. In 1642 it was intended to pay Royalists per week:-
Musketeers - 30d
Dragoons - 64d
Cavalry - 87-1/2d
At the same time they were expected to supply arms and horse themselves. Parliament at first allowed captains £100 mounting money and property owners were expected to supply men and riders from their own pockets. Henry Marten of Shrivenham was engaged to raise six horsemen. With the New Model Army rates of pay were laid down at:-
Foot - 23d
Dragoons - 52d
Cavalry - 70d
The difference now being the Committee hoped to supply mounts, arms and uniforms. Parliament assessed areas according to means and population and local authorities had to levy for the war effort. In 1643 the southern counties were ordered to raise 6,500 horses, an almost impossible task. When towns were overrun there was always the hope of looting. To prevent this the Earl of Essex promised each soldier 60d in lieu when Reading surrendered.

Food and Lodging

Prior to the war one of the most unpopular customs was that of billeting men on the community. It was costed at 4d per night for soldiers passing through or 17 1/2d a week for stopping. In 1627 billeting cost Wokingham parish £3 which they appear to have lost as their claim was never met. (10) During the war the armies lived off the countryside, a practice that Cromwell condemned. Berkshire suffered more than most, having both sides occupying garrisons within the county.

Writers recording their war experiences often recalled the lack of food supplies. Foster wrote of the Gloucester campaign, 'we could get no accommodation either for meat or drink, but what we brought in our snapsacks.' On reaching Swindon he recalled 'we drove along with our army 1000 sheep and 60 head of cattle.... 87 sheep was allotted for our red regiment, but we afterwards lost them all when we came to a fight.' (11) Part of the quartermasters job was to move ahead of the main army and chalk up billets in a town or village. This often led to their death or capture when they were caught unaware and unsupported as at Aldermaston and Newbury.

Wounded

Surgeons and doctors being in short supply were regarded as non combatants and would care for either side after an engagement. On hearing of Hampden's wounds the King made it clear he would send his own surgeon if it would help. During the siege of Reading, Essex had his wounded taken down river in barges to London. Here the first military hospitals in England were established. After the first battle of Newbury the King issued a proclamation which declared in part, 'Though they may be rebels and deserve the punishment of traitors, yet out of our tender compassion upon them, as being our subjects, our will and pleasure is that you carefully provide for their recovery, as well as those of our own army.' (12)

Discipline

It was John Hampden, with fellow colonels, who first drew the attention of the Earl of Essex to the fact that without 'some exemplary punishment' it would be difficult to maintain order in the army. Parliament took up their point and Essex was able to issue 'Laws and Ordinances of War established for the better conduct of the Army'. In 1643 the Royalists published 'Military Orders and Articles established by His Majesty for the better Ordering and Government of His Majestie's Army'. Punishments took the form of loss of pay, whipping, riding a wooden horse, running the gauntlet and shooting or hanging. In cases of the death sentence, often guilty parties would draw lots and only one would be executed. A number of court martials and punishments were carried out at Abingdon and Windsor during the war. (13)

CHAPTER THREE

THE THAMES VALLEY - WINTER 1642-3

The first full battle of the Civil War was fought at Edgehill, Oxfordshire, 23 October 1642. Neither side could justly claim a victory but advantage lay with the King. Urged by his nephew, Prince Rupert, to follow up the advantage with an advance on London, the King hesitated. Cautioned by his older advisers and shocked by the death of so many friends, the King rejected the Prince's suggestion. Six days later the Royal army entered Oxford; the University City was to be the Royal capital for the duration of the war.

On I November, a party of horse from Oxford, riding further than they had intended, approached the outskirts of Reading. Henry Marten MP had garrisoned the town for Parliament.

Marten, a militant opponent of the Court party and later a Republican, had publicly torn up the King's Commission of Array when it was read at Longworth. He provided £1, 200 out of his own pocket towards raising a regiment of horse. Parliament even had to place him in the Tower in August 1643 for stating 'better one family should be destroyed than many', he meant the Royal family. Considered by both sides as a likeable rogue, called a 'great lover of pretty girls' by John Aubrey and 'a whore master' by the King, he was spared from execution by Charles II and imprisoned for life at the Restoration.

On the approach of the Royalist horse towards Reading and hearing conflicting reports of the outcome of Edgehill, Marten abandoned the town 'in great confusion'. The King occupied the town with his army on 4 November.

While the King negotiated with Parliament from Reading, Rupert struck out from Oxford. With a flying column of horse and light artillery, he crossed into Buckinghamshire, stopping to loot the home of Bulstrode Whitelock at Fawley Court, Henley.

On 7 November Rupert summoned Windsor Castle to surrender. Windsor town and the Forest Division of Berkshire held few Royalist supporters. The strict forest laws, the enclosures and prosecutions for poaching made old scores for settling in time of war. Soon after the outbreak of hostilities the Berkshire Militia had occupied the castle where they were soon joined by Colonel Venn and companies of London Trained Bands. Contrary to propaganda Venn had not turned the Chapel into a stable but rather ordered that care should be taken that nothing belonging to the Order of the Garter should be 'defaced.'

Windsor was now 'considered a place of much importance,' for its arsenal and 'to cut off the traffic out of the West to London by stopping their barges there. Rupert set five guns in the grounds of Eton College and had trenches started towards the defences. Rupert managed to penetrate the town whereby Venn had his seven cannon hauled back into the castle. The townspeople followed the cannon in, fearing Rupert's reputation of total war. A Parliament captain was killed as the gates were closed. The light cannon had little effect on the castle walls but Venn's heavier pieces killed five of Rupert's men. The gentlemens sons considered this type of warfare was not their style and complained to Rupert of the duties entailed in digging ditches and attacking fortifications. Realising nothing would be gained at Windsor the Prince withdrew his force to Runnymede allowing some of his men to plunder Staines. The seige of Windsor had lasted eight hours. (2)

While the negotiations were in progress the King made his way slowly towards London, leading his army. On reaching Colnbrook he was reunited with Rupert.

The day after Rupert's abortive attempt on Windsor Castle, the Earl of Essex led his army into London. While Parliament debated the peace overtures they thought fit to order Essex to Hammersmith and Major-General Philip Skippon to muster 6000 men of the London Trained Bands. Mistrust of the King's motives in approaching close to the capital with his army was not misplaced. On the evening of 11 November the King ordered Rupert to attack Brentford at first light.

Denzil Holles's and Lord Brooke's regiments were over-run after a strong defence. Royalist guns were placed in the grounds of Sion House and brought to bear on barges carrying men and ammunition on the river. London acted swiftly to the breach of trust. Essex ordered the regiment guarding Kingston Bridge back into London while throwing a pontoon bridge of boats over the Thames at Putney; now he could operate on both banks of the river. Skippon led the Trained Bands out on to the common at Turnham Green. Behind the old soldier's men came Londoners in their thousands. Old men, women, children and apprentices threw themselves into the task of defending their city. For almost two days the armies faced each other and then slowly the Royal Army drew back. First they moved to Hounslow, then along the same route they had come, they returned to Reading. On 19 November the King re-entered the Berkshire town and for 7 1/2d the ringers of St Mary's were busy 'ringing for the King at his return from Branford after the fight'. Twelve years later they charged four-fold to 'ring for the lord protector.'(3)

It was the custom during this period for armies to go into winter quarters. After Turnham Green the King remained in Reading for a few days and then returned to Oxford. The county now lay in his hands apart from 'that barren division about Windsor'. With Oxford as the new capital and the threat that, winter over, Parliament would go on the offensive, a ring of defence garrisons were established about the city. A Council of War held in Oxford on 9 December decided the quarters for the 'Oxford Army'. (4) Many of the regiments quartered in the county that winter were to see service in Berkshire during the war.

Abingdon

Two regiments of horse under the command of Prince Rupert and Lord Wilmot were stationed at Abingdon. Rupert had 465 men and 63 horses while Wilmot had 355 men and 450 mounts. On 5 December Wilmot led the uncharacteristic winter attack on Marlborough and in February Rupert stormed Cirencester. The foot garrisoned in Abingdon were under Sir Lewis Dyve, in addition there were 30 men and 36 horses 'for the cannon'. The soldiers

ROBERT DEVEREUX EARLE OF ESSEX HIS EXCELLENCY LORD GENERALL OF the forces raised by the Authority of the Parliament For the defence of the King and Kingdom

The Earl of Essex from a contemporary engraving.

were billeted in private homes and St Nicholas's Church was turned into a barracks.

Item for making clene the churche at the first time the souldiers came. xviij d.

item for making clene the churche the second time of the souldiers coming. xviij d. (5)

A few earthworks were started about the town for defence but they were not very elaborate. More attention was given to the bridge over the Thames. A cross-bar of iron which could be raised and lowered and a gate with seven rows of pikes stopped horsemen riding in, leaving only a path for men on foot. Sir Lewis Dyve, appointed governor of Abingdon (6) was soon writing to Prince Rupert on how ill-clothed his men were. He had little money for shoeing horses and was generally low on provisions.

Wallingford

The Royalists quartered one regiment of horse and two of foot in Wallingford. The horse were commanded by Lord Digby and the foot by Thomas Blagge and Earl Rivers. Blagge, made governor, was a Suffolk man as were five of his officers. Many of Rivers' soldiers were recruited in Cheshire. For many, at a time when ones county was also ones country, Berkshire was a foreign land.

Wallingford Castle was fortified 'very strongly with double bulwarks' and two heavy cannon were positioned in the town. A draw-bridge was constructed, probably by breaking down the centre of the river bridge, as was the practice. The only way to enter the town was from the south side. Warrants were sent out that all arms including fowling pieces were to be brought into the castle. All the local ovens were to be employed in baking biscuits for the soldiers rations. Houses close to the castle were demolished and their occupants ordered into the fortress. Lime was brought in from Nettlebed for building work and parts of the castle wall were lowered to allow cannon a better field of fire. Ditches were dug to allow water to run completely round the town and little wicket gates had to be negotiated. The brook from Blewbury was deepened and about a mile from the town a sluice was made that

could easily be pulled up and down either to fill the river or let it run dry. All the houses on the Cholsey and Brightwell side were pulled down and left a line of vision for two miles. (7)

Spies, known as scouts, watched as the garrison was thus prepared against attack. Carriers, carters and other travellers that would not excite suspicion were employed in this dangerous work, many were hanged when captured. The head of the Parliamentary intelligence was Sir Samuel Luke and the reports were laid before him at Windsor. (8) In May 1643 two warrants were received and signed for by Blagge relating to supplies. (9) One was for a load of 10 cwt of powder and the same weight in match and shot, the second was for 7 cwt of match. Luke, within two days of the loads arriving, was able to note, 'That there was a loade of powder, match and bullet carryed from Abingdon to Wallingford guarded with about 30 men'. His spies missed very little in Berkshire that winter.

Faringdon
A regiment of horse, 200 strong and commanded by Rupert's brother Maurice, billeted at Faringdon. They had for company two regiments of dragoons, 500 with Sir Edward Duncombe and 200 commanded by Edward Grey. Grey's whole regiment was captured at Winchester, 12 December 1642, by Sir William Waller. For many their next billet was the prison at Windsor Castle.

Little was done at this time to fortify Faringdon. The officers used Faringdon House as their headquarters. The house was the home of Sir Robert Pye the elder who supported Parliament on the one hand and supplied the King with secret funds with the other. His son, a strong Parliament man had raised his own troop of horse, many recruited locally, and was now in service with the Earl of Essex. After the affair of the Dorsetmen's mutiny it can be imagined how the townspeople took to their new military lodgers.

Reading
The county town became the largest garrison of the 'ring'. Second only to Oxford in the quarter for the Oxford Army, over 3000 soldiers camped in and around the town. The King's military advisers were constantly at odds over the importance of Reading.

Some viewed it as nothing more than a good sized winter quarter too large to defend. Others regarded it as a vital part of Oxford's defence and the key to communications with the west country. According to the December List eight regiments were quartered at Reading.

The horse were under the commands of Sir Arthur Aston, and Sir Thomas Aston, the latter having three troops. The numbers cited for companies and strength indicate how far below the desired requirements they were. Richard Bolle had eight companies, mainly raised in Staffordshire and only 560 strong. Richard Feilding had the same number of companies but only 460 men. Sir Edward Fitton commanded 460 men, mainly raised in Cheshire and divided into eight companies. Henry Lunsford's Somerset men later became Prince Rupert's Bluecoats when the regiment was reorganised. Sir Thomas Salusbury's 'twelve hundred poor Welsh vermin', were the largest Royalist regiment and as the unkind remark indicates came from North Wales. A fellow Welsh regiment was Edward Stradling's, eight companies from South Wales.

Newbury

Newbury was not a Royalist garrison. The town was strongly sympathetic to Parliament and had artfully spread word that plague was rife in the town on the approach of Royalist scouts. At the same time they invited Parliament soldiers secretly into the town. Newbury was the home of the important Puritan Divine, William Twisse. Born in 1578 at Speenhamland he had visions at the age of twelve. Chaplain to the popular Protestant Elizabeth of Bohemia, her son Rupert tried to win him to the King's side. Against the war he sided with Parliament and was nominated to the Westminster Assembly of Divines. Twisse died in 1646 and was given a State funeral and buried in Westminster Abbey. In 1661 his remains were disinterred and thrown into a common pit in St Margaret's Churchyard. (10) Newbury remained loyal to Parliament throughout the war, a fact that Colonel Dalbier urged the Committee of Both Kingdoms not to forget when the town was endangered in 1646. The years of suffering for the people of

Berkshire began that winter. Throughout the war they would either have garrisons billeted in the county or armies marching through. Food, fodder and other provisions had to be found for either sides war effort. Both factions preyed on the countryside, loyalty to the King or Parliament meant very little. Agriculture and trade declined as more and more labourers were pressed into the armies.

Already the King, in a letter penned in Reading, had made it clear to his garrison commanders how they were to be kept supplied. 'And if there shall not be sufficient for such their supply in their quarters, then they are to send forth their warrants to the several hundreds and parishes adjacent, requiring the inhabitants to bring in all fitting provision for their daily support'. (11)

Cattle, horses, sheep and oxen were forcibly taken, one party of Cavaliers removing slow moving oxen from Old Windsor within sight of the castle. Thirty people in Wargrave, assisted by Windsor troopers, stopped Royalists taking five cart loads of wheat and 150 sheep from their village. (12) All bridges, barge ferries and mills along the river Kennet, Loddon and Thames were either broken down or burned. At Wokingham men of the Reading garrison ordered the townspeople to fill eight carts with firewood and bedding. When they failed to meet the demand, four houses were destroyed in reprisal and the occupiers brutally told to 'take themselves to Windsor'. Twyford complained to Parliament that they were being pillaged almost daily by one side or the other.

Both sides tried to regularise systems of contributions from those areas under their control. The King had demanded plate, money and provisions from the counties of Oxfordshire, Buckinghamshire and Berkshire. The High Sheriff of Oxford answered the demand on behalf of Oxon and Berks in a speech to the King in which he did not intend to 'mince the intentions of the divers of the people of these Counties'. He informed the King at Oxford that on the 'question of Money, Plate, or Horses' the county would not be willing to freely give, he went on, 'The greater part of these Counties consist of much tillage and husbandrie, and in that, and in grazing, all the wealth and substance: and for the husband-men and Yeomanrie, they cry out that they are quite undone and ruined, by the dreadful continuation of these wars;

that the souldiers have driven away or killed the Cattell ..... ' But the common voice of the multitude is, that if they never had so much money, then would not part with a penny of it to the maintenace of these wars... These are the votes of the Plebians who either cannot or will not part with a penny towards the maintenance of Your Highnesses wars'. (13) This was followed up by a 'Humble Petition' from the county of Berks for 'a Sudden accomodation of Peace with His Parliament'. (14)

A year before the same people had requested the county be put in a posture of defence, now they complained to the King that while he remained at Oxford, Berkshire would be 'the very theatre where all the tragedies which are derivative from the cruelty and barbarism of such a war as this is, must be acted, since we are exposed, as it were in the very middest, betwixt both armies' 'so long as we behold the best of our towns fortified and stuffed with garrisons, walls and bulwarks being raised, and Ordnance planted, which must needs terrifie the people uninured to such instruments of death and destruction in and about the good town of Reading'.

The fear for Reading lay in the tremendous loss of market trade for all the villages around the busy town. There was also fear of what would happen once the Parliament army was ready to leave Windsor and march on Oxford, perhaps by way of Reading. '... the inhabitants, who are sure to suffer both from the besiegers and the besieged, the same fate being imminent in Abingdon and other good Townes of this Countie, where Your Majesty hath fixed garrisons'. Lord Falkland read the King's answer to the petitioners who met at Oxford. Speaking of the King he said, 'He is not ignorant of the many afflictions hath befallen you since the beginning of these unhappy wars.... for the misdemeanours of his Majesties Souldiers, of which He is altogether ignorant;' He finished the reply by saying the King shared their hopes for a peace.

Meanwhile the war went on. Samuel Luke, Scout Master General, was informed that Sir Arthur Aston, Governor of Reading, was in the habit of dining out in Reading at either

31

Mapledurham or at Mr Englefield's house at White Knights and he might easily be taken. 200 Horse. and 600 foot set out from Windsor on a kidnap attempt. Warned by his own scouts, Aston stayed safely in Reading and at the same time despatched a party to capture a pay cart travelling through the Great Park; his effort also met with failure.

On Sunday 8 January 1643, 320 Royalists led by Captains' Fawcett and Aston, marched to Twyford Green and 'planted two small drakes, and raised a good Brest-work'. There were over 700 Roundheads quartered about Twyford and soon some of their billets came under fire. Captain Turner, a Roundhead officer, led 120 men in a Forlorn Hope attack on the breast-work. After hand to hand fighting, Turner was given support from the reserve forces led by Lord Chomley. Lord Rochford then led an assault on the Cavaliers left wing, forcing them from their positions and back towards Reading. Ten days later Chomley was engaged once more in a skirmish at Hurst. Cavaliers almost took the town at 4 o'clock on the afternoon of the 17th but were once again forced back into their garrison at Reading. (15)

The Earl of Essex, in command of the forced training at Windsor ordered Colonels' Goodwin and Hurry to relieve Marlborough. When the Earl issued their movement Instructions he drew their attention to Newbury, 'a very honest town', where they could either shelter or find assistance. Goodwin missed the main Royalist force returning from their successful attack on Marlborough, but fell on a small party near Wantage. 30 Cavaliers were killed and a further 50 captured, including 6 women. The women were allowed to travel on to Oxford but Goodwin had to destroy the ammunition captured, not having the time to transport it.(16)

Parliament, ruling without its Acts being ratified by the King and Royal Seal, resorted to government by Ordinance or Decree. A number of these were issued which affected Berkshire during the war years and committees were appointed to see the ordinances were carried out. (17) In February 1643, Parliament assessed Berkshire as being able to pay a weekly sum of £550 towards their war effort. To finance the war the Roundheads also resorted to confiscation, or 'sequestering', the estates of 'notorious delinquents'. The Sequestration Ordinance for 1 April 1643 included 'Money, Goods, Chattels, Debts and Personal Estate, as also all and every the Manors, Lands, Tenements, and Hereditaments, rents, arrerages, Revenues and Profits'. Religious persecution was taken care of by an ordinance for the 'act for the Punishment of Scandalous Clergymen and others'. The soldiery could now have licence to attack churches and clergymen on the flimsiest excuse. Committees were instructed to supply the names of any that refused payment towards the military assessment. On 3 August 1643, the county was once more considered able to pay £550 weekly, over a period of two months, for the 'Speedy Raising and Levying of Money for the Maintenance of the Army raised by Parliament and other great affairs of the Commonwealth.' In October a further Ordinance demanded from Berkshire £120 per month for six months, 'For the Relief and Maintenance of sick and maimed Soldiers.' Horses were almost as important as money to both sides and there was soon as shortage of good mounts in the county. On 23 July 1643, Parliament ordered the county to supply 200 'trained', horse, to be delivered to Windsor Castle within three days; an impossible task.

Although the King was to lack control over the civil administration of the county during the war years, his military arm was quite capable of enforcing any levy he might make on the area. In this way the inhabitants suffered twice in all matters of keeping both armed forces supplied. A Royalist Council of War held on 13 October 1643, and attended by the King, drew up an agreement for the Berkshire representatives, which left little room for argument. The knights, gentlemen, freeholders and inhabitants of the county were called upon to supply and provision the Royal Oxford Army. This was to be done in the form of a loan of £1000 per week, an enormous sum for the period, made worse by Parliament's demands of another £550. The hundreds of Bray,  Cookham, Benhurst and Wargrave were cynically exempt, they were too near Windsor Castle for the Royalists either to collect or to exact reprisals for non-compliance. At the same time the county was expected to make good the difference lost by these hundreds. The agreement called for the levy to be met, half in cash, half in provisions. Any attempt to avoid the full levy by increasing food prices was prevented by setting an established figure on certain items. Oats were rated at 20d a bushell, beans and peas at 3d a bushell, hay 5d the todde, grass for one horse at 3s a week and straw at 10s a load. A pernicious clause stated that should property or livestock be lost or damaged by the soldiery, then the cost would come out of the loan they were already paying. The supplies were to be delivered, at the county's expense to Abingdon, every Friday. Billeting was to be paid for but camp followers, women and children, could not be housed without the tenants permission. The conditions of the agreement were ordered to be posted in every church and chapel in the county. (18)

It was not until August 1645 that the ordinary villagers and townspeople of the county at last called 'enough' to the demands of both sides. They formed a 'Clubman' association along with other western counties and petitioned against the demands made by the King and Parliament. Thousands gathered on Compton Down to protest and to hear the declaration read, calling for a just and peaceful end to the war. All this lay in the future, in the winter of 1642 to 1643, the county's suffering had hardly begun.

CHAPTER FOUR

WINDSOR - WINTER 1642-3

'Stone Walls do not a Prison make,
Nor Iron bars a Cage;'
Richard Lovelace.

As the two armies met at Edgehill, Sir John Seyton, with a party of Berkshire militia, occupied Windsor Castle. Captain Fog ordered that the doors of the treasury should be opened. When informed that it needed three keys which were not immediately available, Fog sent for iron bars to break in the door. Plate and other valuables were removed to London.(1) While Seyton took the initiative, the Commons advised the Committee for Defence of the Kingdom, 'to take special care of Windsor Castle'.

Twelve companies from the London Trained Bands, under Colonel John Venn, marched into Windsor on 28 October 1642. In London printed reports of the occupation of the castle were already selling on the streets.

'Severall Troopes of Dragooners and Volunteers, some of which are arrived already at Windsor, and have taken possession of the Castle for the use of his Majesty and Parliament, others are in their march towards Windsor, where being arrived, they intend to fortefie themselves and to make out-workes, ...'(2)

It was these 'out-workes' that within a few days Rupert's men were attacking. After Rupert drew off to Runnymede the propagandists were able to write, 'Colonel Venn behaved himself very bravely, to the wonder and amazement of the beholders. '(3)

Colonel John Venn was fifty-six when he took command of Windsor Castle, later he was appointed governor. A past Warden of the Merchant Taylors Company, he was a member of the Artillery Company, progressing from captain to colonel. In 1640 he had been a burgess for the City of London and he was

Westminster at the time of the Civil War.

already a trusted Parliament man. Venn remained governor of
Windsor until 1645 when he was replaced by another Londoner,
Christopher Whichcott, of the Green Auxiliaries. During his time
in Berkshire, Venn served on a number of county committees.
Later he attended all but two sittings of the King's trial and was a
signator to the Death Warrant. Had he not died in bed in 1650 it
is almost certain he would have faced execution as a Regicide. (4)
Venn's chaplain at Windsor was Christopher Love. A Puritan, he
grew disillusioned with the extremists in his party and was
executed for corresponding with Queen Henriette Marie.

One of Venn's company captains at Windsor was John Barkstead,
a London goldsmith. Barkstead was to have strong associations
with Berkshire, he eventually became governor of Reading. was
promoted colonel of his own regiment and narrowly escaped
being captured by Royalists in April 1645. Riding along the
Reading to Newbury road he was surprised by a party of horse
operating from Wallingford. Barkstead attended all the sittings of
the trial and signed the warrant. Betrayed when hiding on the
continent he was brought back to England and executed as a
Regicide. (5)

Windsor Castle figured prominently in the war events. Parliament
used the castle and park as the training ground for their army.

When the army became all-powerful, the castle became the meeting place of the Grandees. Sadly it was also the prison and burial place of the King.

The castle was far too small to house all the troops and houses were taken over in the town. Years later the inn-keepers petitioned for the money owed them for billeting, 16, 8, 1 0, or 12 in a house, 'to whom they have to lend 6d a day and allow fire, candle, dressing for food, and lodging...' (6)

The shortage of food and firewood led to the deer herds-and parks pales disappearing at an alarming rate. 'That my Lord General (making his first winter quarters at Windsor) his soldiers destroyed all the Deer of the said Park, being above 500, and burnt up all the pales..' said a petitioner. (7)

The religious extremists soon turned their attentions on the Chapel in the castle and the churches in the town. Plate, brass images, the enamels from Wolsey's unfinished tomb and other objects of value were removed from the castle. A great deal of plate went to be melted down for coining to pay the army. Venn was instructed to remove 'scandalous monuments and pictures in execution in the several churches and chapels at Windsor and Eton...'. It is fair to say however that some of the reports of damage to the Chapel have been exaggerated. It has been claimed windows were broken, woodwork ripped out and the body of the chapel used as a stable, details of which cannot be substantiated. (8) In fact Venn was ordered to **take** special care of materials relating to the Garter and its Chapel. He was ordered to seize and sequester the local estates of 'Papists, Bishops. Deans, Deans and Chapters and notorious delinquents... in the Town of Windsor..'. Dean Wren, Registrar of the Order of the Garter died shortly after. Few of the canons expelled lived long enough to be restored.

It did not take Parliament long to realise that in Windsor Castle they had an ideal prison suitable for 'ill-affected and very dangerous persons.' Word soon spread of known Royalist sympathisers being 'fetched out of their beds... and hurried away to Windsor Castle.' Included among the first prisoners confined at Windsor were two high sheriffs, Sir Francis Doddington of Somerset and Sir Edward Fortescue of Devon. Both had been arrested for reading the King's Commission of Array. Brought to Windsor in January 1643, both effected an escape a few months later. With the two sheriffs were a number of officers taken at Winchester and Chichester.

'... the said Colonel, his deputy, or assigns shall or may, from time to time receive and take of every Lieutenant, Cornet, or Ensign, twentysix shillings and eightpence, and not above, at his or their entrance', 'inferior officer or ordinary person 20s' 'Knight, Captain of Horse or Foot or Esquire. 40s.' 'Colonel, Lieutenant Colonel, Sergeant Major or any Person of High Degree, 5 marks.'

Early in January Parliament decided to remove some sixty prisoners from various confinements in London to the security of Windsor. At first it was suggested they pay for their own transport but eventually Venn was allowed £20 for coaches. A further £50 was given to him to make improvements to their accommodation. 55 prisoners made up the first batch and on arrival they were placed in various parts of the castle. The conditions in which they were confined could be eased by payment for extras, as it was they were charged an 'entry-fee' to their prison. Venn was given a scale of charges that had to be collected on their arrival, nothing is said of what he should do if they could not pay.

A later prisoner, Thomas Knyvett, wrote to his wife describing conditions for prisoners of his rank and station.
'... We have but two rooms for 7 of us the first night, and one bed for all of us. I hope you will now say we lay like pigs-hogs indeed..'

As the war progressed the castle began to fill up with the ordinary prisoners of war, conditions for the lower orders were 'pig-hog' indeed. Brought by coach or by barge they were herded together. Straw was issued for sleeping on and 3d (1 1/2p) a day was allowed for each to provide beer, biscuits, cheese and butter. A surgeon was appointed to care for the wounded but the conditions made the mortality rate high. In one instance the Marshall was given £3. 1. 8. 'for shrouds to bury 30 common soldiers which died in prison.' (9)

CHAPTER FIVE

THE SIEGE OF READING - APRIL 1643.

The King appointed Sir Arthur Aston, governor of Reading. His salary was set at £7 per week, payable by the inhabitants. Aston, a Catholic and strict disciplinarian, was unpopular with his men and hated by the opposition. 'Wednesday last, Colonel Aston feasted the Magistrates of Reading and hanged a man or two' wrote a Parliamentarian. He had in fact authorised the execution of a man named Boyes, a Londoner, found guilty of spying. The register of St Laurencels Church records, 'December 10 a parliament soldier executed.'

Aston had past military experience and he used this in his efforts to fortify the town. If we are to believe Clarendon, this was to be sufficient for the winter quarter, the town to be abandoned by April 1643. According to a Council of War held at Oxford, come the spring the defences of Reading would be destroyed and the garrison drawn out as a field army.

Leading townsmen were ordered to 'work in raising the bulwarks in Forbury, on pain of forfeiting seven pence a day for every days non attendance, out of which fines the poorer sort were to be allowed eight pence a day for their labor'. The earthworks eventually became as 'high as a house'. These earthen redoubts were built at Forbury, Harrison's Barn and at the end of Pangbourne Lane.

The remains of the Forbury redoubt can still be seen in Forbury Gardens, other named forts are harder to identify with certainty. 'Fort Royal' could have been another name for Forbury but is more likely to have been a redoubt in the area of Castle Street. 'Fort Invincible' and Harrison's Barn are thought to be one and the same place, and stood in Battle Street. Pangbourne Lane was the part of Oxford Road immediately joining Broad Street.

Cannons were brought in from the Oxford magazine. At one time there were five in the

Market Place, two at the end of Friar Street, two in Broad Street and one placed in the top of St Mary's Church. Other cannon were set up in the grounds of the Abbey and on bridges and roads leading into the town.

Caversham, with its river bridge, was considered an important defensive outpost. Earthworks went up on Caversham Heights, around the church and by the bridge. The centre of the bridge was pulled up and replaced with a drawbridge. On market days this was supplemented with planks of wood to enable the heavy carts to cross, at night these were thrown into the river.

A great broad ditch was 'cast about the towne from Fryers Corner to St Laurence Church.' Guard posts, including one in the Oracle were supplied with food and firewood at the town's expense. Another fort was built south of the town 'against Dowles Green and a breastwork from it to Harrison's Barn guarded by sentrys to hinder any movement from Shinfield to Reading.' The open fields to the east were 'sown with iron engines' to impede horses. All roads into Reading were ditched and draw-bridged. Posts were fixed in rows at the end of each street and chains slung between them, the road surface was deliberately pot-holed.

Oxford and Newbury were ordered to supply hundreds of shovels, mattocks and picks, for digging the trenches. Match, ammunition, powder and arms poured into Reading by cart and barge. Already a shortage of powder was beginning to concern the defenders.

All the available wool in the town, plus that being transported through the town by carriers, was appropriated and used for wool packs. Like a modern sandbag, the defenders would fire from behind them. Pebbles were dredged from the Thames and tipped into wicker-work baskets called gabions, behind these the gun platforms were built. Fodder and food supplies were brought in daily and it was forbidden to take out certain commodities such as wheat and rye. Trade with London by Reading merchants was prohibited by Royal Ordinance.

After the Royalist victory at Cirencester the prisoners taken were brought to Reading. It was suggested that one in five should be pressed into Royal service in the garrison. Aston acidly answered the idea by saying 'he had enemies enough without the King sending him more. '

A regiment was raised in the town by impressment. The men soon deserted, they claimed through lack of pay. Aston levied a contribution from householders of £102 to pay those that remained and the householders petitioned the King that they had already parted with thousands for Aston's use. The King's answer was to instruct Aston to raise another £2000 and leading townsmen were forced to mortgage their properties.

'Suspect Malignants' were thrown out of their churches. Puritans, Presbyterian and other anti-Laudians (he was still in the Tower) were labelled malignants. One resident of Reading was Christopher Milton, brother to John Milton, the poet. Christopher was a staunch Royalist and he was forced to leave Reading with the army when the town capitulated. Old Sir Francis Knollys, known as 'the ancient Parliament man in England', he was over ninety, represented the town in Parliament and opposed the King. His houses and tenants were made to suffer for his allegiance.

Parliamentary scouts reported almost daily on the progress of the defences and through them some parties in the town indicated they would welcome a Parliamentary advance, they even promised aid should an attempt be made on Reading.

In January 1643 the Earl of Essex was ready to open the campaign which, it was fondly hoped, would end at the gates of Oxford and bring peace. A surprise attack on Henley forced the Royalists out and Essex had the town occupied by a large force. The King's military advisers interpreted the taking of Henley as a prelude to a direct move against Oxford which would bypass and isolate Reading. A night counter attack on Henley failed and Essex was able to establish the riverside town as a stepping-stone to Reading. (1)

'Good and true Newes FROM REDDING' declared the banner headline of the tract which went on, 'We have now at last quitted our old quarters, and hope to give the world notice, it

41

was reason and judgement that kept us so long at Windsore, and not cowardice, or ill-will to the Cause;' (2)

Three months after taking Henley, passing by way of Henley, Wargrave and Binfield Heath, mending broken bridges as they went, the 18,000 strong army advanced rapidly on Reading. 'Fifteen April late at night we sate down before Reading, being Saturday at night,' said 'A true Relation. . '

The Earl of Essex 'summoned the towne for the King and Parliament, but Aston the Governour (a Papist and one that is guilty of divers murders) answered very resolutely, He would keep the town or starve in it, ... '

Essex divided his army into two parts, one part attacked Mapledurham House and the redoubts on Caversham Heights. Surprised by the force of the attack, the defenders fell back to the defences about Caversham Church. Cannons were hauled forward and brought to bear on the church and when the steeple sustained a direct hit, the defenders retreated again. Despite a stout last defence around the bridge the odds overwhelmed the Royalists. Essex's troops swept over the bridge and consolidated in the fields now bounded by Cow Lane and Richfield Avenue.

The Earl was now faced with the first siege of the war with newly raised men. A Council of War decided that further storming would be dangerous to their morale and adopted the more careful approach. Entrenching towards the enemy lines was put in the hands of Philip Skippon. Heavier cannon were brought up, including two of the heaviest in the country from the Tower of London armoury. The bombardment began and one of the first casualties was 'Lieutenant Colonel D'Ews, a young man of notable courage and vivacity, who had his leg shot off by a cannon bullett, of which he speedily and very cheerfully died. '

As the trenches got nearer to the town walls, their occupants came under fire. To give themselves cover the trench diggers fired nearby farm buildings. On the Newbury side of town, smoke for cover was not required, (the defenders had failed to remove the hedges.) Well protected the Roundheads approached Harrison's Barn.

On Tuesday Royalist horse appeared on Caversham Heights. They by-passed Reading and at Sonning loaded barges with supplies and 600 musketeers. The barges managed to get safely into Reading and Essex planted batteries along the river bank to prevent it happening again. On the same day Sir Anthony St John's eldest captain was hurt when a cannon exploded. Four men were killed and a dozen wounded in the blast.

Lord Grey arrived with reinforcements for Essex. 'Three regiments of foot; two consisting of 700 a-piece; two troops of dragoons; three pieces of ordnance; which begirt the enemy round from Sonning to Cawsom, Northward and Southward.' Aston, on seeing the town completely surrounded, offered to surrender provided '... he might march away with bag and baggage.' Essex refused the terms, 'we came for the men, not the town.' was his uncompromising reply.

It may have been coincidence, but on the day the town was encircled and Essex was reinforced, Aston was injured. Charitably perhaps, it was recorded that Aston was in a guard room nearest the fighting when injured, most accounts say he was struck by a falling tile, dislodged by cannon fire, when walking in the Abbey grounds. At first it was rumoured he was dead but later, regretfully in tone, a Parliamentarian declared only that he had his 'pate broke.' Aston's wound rendered him incapable of command and the 'eldest colonel', Richard Feilding, assumed control.

By Wednesday, the cannon set up in the church tower had been brought down and St Giles Church badly hit. Sickness however was spreading fast in the ranks of the besiegers. The unhealthy conditions of the camps by the river caused hundreds of soldiers to be shipped down river to the London hospitals. Sick and wounded were moved out of the area daily in carts and barges and Essex was said to have ordered secret burial pits dug well away from the town. Inside Reading a few soldiers were given a burial service, an entry in the register of St Laurence's Church reads, '1643 April 15 to 30th, being the time of the siege, 10 soldiers killed in fight.'

On Thursday, 'two regiments of foote under command of Coll. Boulstrode, Lt-coll Aldridge, and Lt-coll Martin, and five troopes of horse under the command of Major Gunter...' covered the approach of more cannon moved close into the walls. By friday guns were within pistol shot of the Gallows Field bulwarks. Lieutenant Colonel Martin (or Marten) was Henry Marten, last seen hurriedly leaving Reading.

Feilding, on taking command of Reading, made his first duty to send a messenger to Oxford to inform the King that he could only hope to hold out for another week. Aware that should Reading fall he would lose a small army, the King reacted instantly. A relief force was mustered and Rupert, currently besieging Lichfield, was ordered to come to the King as soon as possible. The Prince stormed Lichfield successfully on Friday 21 April and immediately set out for Oxford. By the time he arrived in the city, the King had left for Wallingford, the first stage of the Reading relief.

On receiving Feilding's despatch Charles instructed a servant to Sir Lewis Dyve named Flower, to return into Reading with a message. Feilding was ordered to hold the town until help arrived. Powder and ammunition were promised, brought by an escort of nearly 2000 horse.

Flower managed to swim into Reading but on a return journey he was dragged from the Thames by a Bluecoat drummer. Forced to disclose his information, Flower was thrown into a room with another agent, caught attempting to blow up a magazine, for which he had been paid 10 shillings.

Essex sent a strong party of horse towards Wallingford with orders to harry and delay the Royalist advance. Lord Grey moved his cannon within pistol shot of Harrison's Barn and awaited instructions for blasting the redoubt. The foot were all alerted to watch for any attempted breakout.

Colonels' Barclay and Holborne, lying in wait at Caversham, ambushed part of the supply column.(3) The main body of Roundhead horse reached Wallingford and found the town empty of Royalist horse. Emboldened by this discovery they pressed on towards Dorchester. More by accident than design, they met several hundred Royalist horse in narrow Dorchester. The Royalists on their part were totally unprepared for their visitors and the Roundheads, left no alternative, charged. The result was a complete rout for the King's men, which included his own troop. A number were killed, wounded or captured and the Royal Colour was taken. Triumphantly the victors returned to Reading with their prisoners and trophy. (4)

It may have been this unexpected and small skirmish that gave Reading and its defenders to Parliament. Historians have argued as to why, at about 9 a.m. on the morning of 25 April, Feilding ordered a white flag to be hung out for negotiations to begin. With the King and Rupert so near why should this gallant commander capitulate? Although it cannot be proved and did not appear to have arisen at his court martial, did Feilding see the captured Royal Colour? Did he have reason to believe that the relief force had been destroyed - it can only be conjecture. At his trial Rupert interceded on his behalf and Feilding served with distinction in later battles.

In any event, the truce flag was shown at the same time as the King, now joined by Rupert, appeared on Caversham Heights. 40 colours were carried, nine regiments of foot and at least three regiments of horse, fell on Caversham Bridge. Peter Young, eminent Civil War historian, suggests the regiments included, Colonel John Owen's, Herbert's, Innis's, Sir Gilbert Gerard's, Lord Molyneux's, Lord Forth's, Sir Ralph Dutton's and perhaps one (5) regiment from Oxford and one from Wallingford. Sir Lewis Dyve's were in the forefront.

Little use could be made of the artillery in the driving rain and sleet. Rupert's forces were driven back and the Prince was furious with the garrison for not launching a counter move from the town. Some inhabitants claimed later they had witnessed officers in the town beating their men forward and the soldiers begging, 'doe not kill us before we see our enemies.' The Royalist attack only resulted in a few carts getting through and messengers coming out to inform

the Prince that Colonel Bowles, Lieutenant Colonel Thewell and Major Gilbey were hostages for the Royalists good intent while negotiations were under way.

With the Royal army massing before the town and fresh powder inside, some officers urged Feilding to break the truce. This he adamantly refused to consider saying, '...if the King himself come knock at the gates, and command him to do it, he would not forfeit his honour.'
It was agreed that Feilding be allowed to ride from the town and see the King. After the strained interview, the King assented to the terms Feilding had ably negotiated. Essex would 'not have the men' as he had steadfastly told Aston, only the town. On Thursday 27 April the Articles were formally signed, they included:-

'I. That the governor, commanders, and soldiers, both horse and foot, may march out with colours flying, armes and four peeces of ordinance, ammunition, bag and baggage, light match, bullet in mouth, drum beating, and trumpet sounding.... '

'IV. That they have fifty carts for baggage, sick and hurt men, and that they carry not out of the town of Redding, any such goods and commodities as have been taken from the western carriers, and brought into Redding. '

The articles were signed by Richard Feilding, Anthony Thewell, John Belasyes, Theophilus Gilby, Richard Bolle, George Bond and Edward Villiers. The Royalists had saved an army, Feilding had earned a court martial and never held command again.

The Earl of Essex promised his men 12 shillings each in lieu of plunder, an expected bonus as the town had first refused to surrender. The Royalists were attacked however as they left the town under the pretext that they carried an extra 140 muskets in their waggons. This breach of terms was to embitter future engagements and was long remembered by the Royalists. The Earl personally rode into the looters with drawn sword and beat them off.

The two armies passed each other at Friars Corner, the losers marching out, the victors in. 'Colonel Aston came first out in a horselitter, covered with red and lined with white...' His faculties wonderfully restored he led his men 'towards Oxford, by Casum Church. '

Essex's possession of Reading was of a short duration. His army, already sick in their hundreds, experienced an epidemic once billeted in the town. In June he was forced to abandon the place to the Royalists.

CHAPTER SIX

THE FIRST BATTLE OF NEWBURY - SEPTEMBER 1643

At the end of July 1643, much of the west and south-west of England was under the King's control. Parliament had suffered a number of military reverses that summer. John Hampden had been mortally wounded at Chalgrove Field, (18 June), during a skirmish with Prince Rupert's cavalry. One version of Hampden's death wound is that a pistol, given him by his son-in-law Robert Pye, had exploded in his hand. In fact he had been badly wounded in the shoulder and died a few days later. Sir William Waller had been defeated at Lansdown by Lord Hopton, (5 July) and a few days later, (13 July) his army was destroyed at Roundway Down by the combined forces of Hopton, Wilmot and Prince Maurice. Bristol, a vital port for bringing in supplies from the continent, fell to Prince Rupert (26 July), after a bloody storming. On 10 August the victorious King turned his attention on Gloucester and summoned the town to surrender.

Command of this important Parliament stronghold would secure the west for the Royalists. It would ensure free passage out of Wales for reinforcements. Such additions to his man-power would allow the King to march once more on London.

Mindful of the fearful casualties at the storming of Bristol, the King would not permit another costly assault but settled down for a siege. Time, a much needed commodity for Parliament which was locked in political argument over the conduct of the war, enabled a relief force to be assembled.

Under the leadership of Robert, Earl of Essex, a Parliamentary army was formed, reinforced by five regiments of the London Trained Bands. Some of the regiments had seen service at Edgehill and Reading, a few were untried in battle. Twenty regiments of foot and ten of horse were brought together excluding the Trained Bands. A review of the army was held on Hounslow Heath for members of Parliament on 24 August and the noble Earl boldly declared, 'I am tomorrow, God willing, beginning my march, and if the army be as willing to march as I shall be to lead them, and the town should not hold out until we can release them, I shall endeavour it, or perish in the act.'

The Earl may well have been questioning the readiness of the new army to march. According to some accounts the methods used in recruiting the soldiers had caused daily riots in London. Men were dragged from their beds, it was claimed, and many being transported by water to the musters, threw themselves from the barges. Those marching to Hounslow and other rendezvous were escorted by strong bodies of horse to prevent desertion. The readiness of the London Trained Bands to serve so far away from their homes counteracts some of this propaganda, which appeared in Mercurius Aulicus, a Royalist newspaper. (1) But there certainly was impressment needed to make up the army. An Ordinance of 10 August gave powers to the deputy lieutenants of the counties and the militia committee in London, to conscript men and fine or imprison any that refused.

Their willingness to march, through countryside wasted or controlled by Royalists, must have been in question. The army moved off by way of Beaconsfield and Aylesbury, to a rendezvous at Brackley Heath on 1 September. At Brackley Heath the main body was joined by the Train of Artillery and the five London regiments in their red, orange and blue coats. With the Londoners was a strong contingent of horse, almost a regiment strong. They had left the capital to the cheers of the populace, an Ordinance had been passed requiring all London shops to close until Gloucester be relieved.

It is thanks to a sergeant named Foster, serving with the Red Regiment, that we know so much about the Gloucester expedition and the subsequent battle at Newbury. He was author of the grand sounding 'A true and exact Relation of the Marchings of the Two Regiments of the Trained Bands of the City of London, being the Red and Blew Regiments. As also, Of the Three Regiments of the Auxiliary Forces, the Blew, Red and Orange, who marched forth for the reliefe of the City of Glocester, from August 23 to Sept. 28. '(2)

Keeping north of Oxford, the army moved on to Aynho, Adderbury, Chipping Norton to Stow-on-the-Wold. At Stow, Rupert made an attempt to stop the 15,000 strong army but was driven off. On 5 September Essex reached the River Severn and he ordered cannons to be fired for Gloucester to hear and realise help was near. The King, not wishing to face an army with an unsubdued garrison at his rear, abandoned his mines and trenches. His troops were quite happy to leave the mud and squalor of ditches, running in water from the torrential rain that characterised that summer.

On 8 September Essex led his army into the city, the defenders were down to their last three barrels of powder. Gloucester had been saved for Parliament but now the Earl had to return to London and between him and the capital stood a large Royalist army. Parliament had saved a town, now they could lose an army.

Two days later, leaving powder, shot, match, cheese and other supplies, Essex led his army out of Gloucester towards Tewksbury. In an attempt to mislead the King the Earl remained at Tewsbury for four days. His men spent their time constructing a bridge of boats over the Severn, giving the impression that they were on the offensive in the direction of Wales.

During the night of Friday 15 September, Essex turned about and hurried his army south towards Cirencester. Sometime between one and three in the morning, musketeers, led by Sir Robert Pye, attacked Royalist sentries outside Cirencester. They rushed into the town, surprising the troops in their beds, and capturing much needed food supplies. Over 200 prisoners were taken and the Roundheads were forced to use their match to bind them. Twentyseven wagon loads of provisions were looted from the schoolhouse which was the storehouse for the area. A number of horses were captured and used as replacement mounts. There were few casualties on either side although Pye had been wounded in the arm.

The King and Rupert were soon acquainted with Essex's night movement and his success at Cirencester. The King placed the main body of his army on a parallel course with Essex and Rupert led a flying column of horse to intercept. They rightly guessed that

Essex had the intention of returning to London on a route south of the Oxford garrisons. Rupert made for Faringdon via Fairfield and Lechlade and arrived there as the Roundheads marched into Swindon. Sunday, 17 September, was spent in the open fields around Swindon. The days rain gave way to a cold, hard and very frosty night.

On quitting Swindon the Parliamentary army marched strung out between Chiseldon and Aldbourne. Near Dudmore Lodge Rupert struck the rear of the column. With difficulty Sir Philip Stapleton, commanding Essex's Lifeguard, managed to fall back along the column from his position in the van, and eventually drive off the Royalists. (3) Rupert fully appreciated that he lacked the strength to bring Essex to battle but he had delayed him and, more important, diverted his course.

The action at Aldbourne Chase decided Essex to place the River Kennet between his army and that of the King's and Rupert. That night he quartered in Hungerford and again his men encamped in the open fields. The Royalists enjoyed the shelter of Wantage, the King first dining at Faringdon and then moving on to stay the night at the home of Sir George Wilmot at Chariton, near Wantage.

The morning of 19 September dawned wet and chill. The persistent rain had made the narrow lanes and close hedged fields between Hungerford and Newbury heavy with mud. The appalling weather made any progress by a large army, with heavy guns, a slow crawl.

Newbury, with its shelter, food and fresh supplies, became a key point for both sides. Essex saw it as a resting place before seeking the shelter of Reading and his eventual return to London. Quartermasters were sent on in advance to chalk up billets for the soldiery in and around Newbury. Rupert, never slow to assess a military situation, sent a squadron of horse from Lambourn to Newbury and proposed the King move the foot in that direction. With the King's and Rupert's forces combined their army would number that of the

51

Lucius Carey, 2nd Viscount Falkland, killed at the first battle of Newbury. From a portrait attributed to A. Van Dyke.

enemy. The Royal Train of Artillery amounted to some twenty guns.

That morning, a Tuesday, as the quartermasters marked up the billets, cavalry led by Rupert swept into Newbury. Some Roundheads were killed, a few captured and a number died in the streets of the little town. Rupert consolidated the position and awaited the King's arrival with the main army which arrived soon after.

Essex was now left with little room to manoeuvre; a friendly town was secured against him, a strong, relatively fresh army, blocked his path and his tired and hungry soldiers faced another night bivouaced in open fields. Foster described the conditions, 'We were much distressed, for want of sleep as also for other sustenance. It was a night of much rain and we were wet to the skin.'

There was an incident that day that reflects the superstition prevalent at the time. Some of the Earl's soldiers gathered nuts and berries along the river bank. While doing so they saw an old woman 'treading on the water'. It appears she was riding a wooden board in the shallows. Horseplay at her expense seems to have got out of hand and the poor woman was shot with a carbine. Wounded, the soldiers finished their quarry off by a pistol shot, a sword thrust and finally by blowing her brains out with a shot under the ear. Later the barbaric incident was wrapped up in an allegation of witchcraft. The bullets they fired were caught in her hands, or so they claimed. One ball rebounded from her breast and the sword blade turned in her body. Later a pamphlet described the affair as 'A MOST certain strange and true discovery of a Witch.'(4) When brought before their officers the men claimed that the woman's dying words justified their murdering her, 'And is it come to pass that I must dye indeed, why then his Excellencie the Earle of Essex shall be fortunate and win the field'. Perhaps the alleged words failed to comfort the Earl when he retired to bed that night at Biggs Cottage - his ghost is said to haunt the place.

The Parliament army had approached

Newbury from Hungerford through the villages of Kintbury and Enborne. The artillery train was drawn into the shelter of Hamstead Park and the army was deployed on a line from the Kennet to the edge of Crockham Heath. John Middleton's horse were fronted by the foot under Lord Robartes, they covered the Kennet flank. Philip Skippon commanded the centre with the Trained Bands held in reserve to his rear. Sir Philip Stapleton controlled the right.

While the King settled down for a comfortable night in Newbury his army deployed in a line face on to the Roundheads. The Earl of Carnarvon is said to have made a show of measuring the width of a gateway into Newbury. When asked the purpose of his labour he laughingly replied that he was concerned lest the Earl of Essex's horns would leave enough room to let him pass as a prisoner. (horns on a man then meant that he was a cuckolded husband, Essex had been far from successful in matrimony.)

Sir Gilbert Gerard took the left wing facing Stapleton and next to him were Prince Rupert's cavalry. Between the Prince and Sir Nicholas Byron, just to their front, were placed batteries of cannon. (slightly north west of the Falkland Memorial). Sir John Byron and Sir Thomas Aston faced the Roundhead centre towards Skinners Green. On the far right of the Royalist battle line, against the Kennet, lay Sir William Vavasour.

Although the Royalists held the advantage of the higher terrain of Wash Common, one vital feature had been overlooked. Either carelessness or the lateness of the hour with gathering darkness, caused them to overlook that Wash Common plateau contained a spur that juts out commanding a large tract of ground towards the Kennet. A spur that, viewed from the Roundhead lines on Skinner's Green and towards Enborne, took on the appearance of a 'round hill'. Byron wrote later, 'Here another error was committed, and that a most gross and absurd one, in not viewing the ground, although we had day enough to have done it, and not possessing ourselves of those hills above the town by which the enemy was necessarily to march the next day to Reading.' (5) This natural feature was to become a focal point in the battle and the 'Round Hill' or 'Bigg's Hill' of the contemporary accounts.

During the morning twilight hours of 20 September, Robert, Earl of Essex, wearing a conspicuous broadbrimmed white hat, rode through the ranks of his waking soldiers. He had little in the way of comforting words to give them, 'They hold the hill, the town, hedges, lane and river', he told them. While Essex did his rounds, Skippon and a number of pioneers were hauling two guns up the slope of Round Hill. Reaching the brow, they discovered to their surprise, that it was unoccupied by the Royalists. Hurriedly they set to sighting their guns on the campfires of their enemy. When daylight broke Skippon's artillery men opened fire on the cavalry, foot and Royalist guns drawn up in their batteries.

The situation left Essex with no alternative other than to go on the offensive. Battle was joined on both wings with the Royalists enjoying all the early successes. In the centre all efforts to dislodge Skippon met with stiff resistance and heavy casualties. The battle area had at that time a number of hedges dividing off small fields. The intersecting lanes were extremely narrow and steep banked. In these conditions cavalry movement was severely hampered.

Slowly the battle centred on Round Hill and the Wash Common area. The artillery duel between Skippon's guns on Round Hill and the King's batteries sited near the present Gun public house, added black palls of smoke to the confusion of the milling combatants.

Royalist pikemen and musketeers were ordered in front of the cavalry to rip down the hedges and riders dismounted to assist them. Once the gaps were made the cavalry were able to attempt some free movement in the next field. It was while negotiating one of these gaps, and spurring his horse headlong through, that Lord Falkland was killed.

Lord Falkland, the King's reluctant Secretary of State, was serving with Sir John Byron. It is said that he deliberately courted death at Newbury. Clarendon wrote of him, 'But from the entrance into this unnatural war, his natural cheerfulness and vivacity grew clouded, and a kind of sadness and dejection of spirit stole upon him which he had never been used to.' It is one of the ironies of civil war that prior to the battle, Twisse, the Puritan Roundhead, administered the Sacrament to Falkland the cavalier.

Slowly the defenders of the Round Hill position were driven back by the combined efforts of Sir John Byron and Aston's horses, supported by the foot of Colonel Wentworth and Lisle. Moving back with their guns, Skippon's men retired as far as Skinner's Green Lane. There the resistance was stiffened by the reserve London Trained Bands. Clarendon described their steadfast defence, 'The London train-bands and auxiliary regiments (of whose inexperience of danger, or any kind of service beyond the easy practice of, their postures in the Artillery Garden, men had till then too cheap an estimation) behaved themselves to wonder, and were in truth the preservation of that army that day.' Henry Foster wrote, '... we lost sixty or seventy men in our Red Regiment of the Trained Bands, besides wounded men; we having the hottest charge from the enemy's cannon of any regiment in the army.'

Round Hill was retaken and Skippon was able to reinforce the position with even heavier guns. 'The fight continued without intermission all that day,' said one observer. In fact skirmishing continued into the early hours of the next day.

As night fell the King called a Council of War. Some of the officers present voted to retain their positions ready to continue the struggle at dawn. One of the leading advocates against such a proposal was Lord Percy, General of Ordnance. He pointed out that much of the powder and ammunition for the cannon had been used up. Eighty barrels of powder had been expended, twenty more than at Edgehill the previous year. A Parliament witness to the battle had noted the Royalists were only firing one shot for every three of his at the close of day. Lord Percy and his faction had their way, during the early hours of darkness the army and train were drawn away towards Oxford.

As dawn broke the weary Parliament forces prepared once more to attempt a breakthrough. After a few cannon shots and tentative scouting it was reported to Essex that the field was theirs.

But at what cost to both sides? Foster counted 100 bodies about his own position, many laying stripped naked in the mud. The ghouls, ever present near a battlefield, had crept forward about their ghastly business under cover of darkness. Later, townspeople told Foster the King had taken 30 cart loads of dead and wounded when he left. That day Foster saw 20 more carts filled with dead and witnessed 30 bodies thrown into one pit and 14 buried in a ditch where they fell.

In addition to Falkland the King had lost Lord Carnarvon, Lord Sunderland and many other senior officers. One Berkshire Royalist killed at Newbury was Algernon Simes of Little Park Windsor. He served with Sir Richard Harrison of Hurst who, with his brother-in-law, Richard Beavor of Binfield, raised three troops of horse for the King.

Slowly Essex and his officers gathered their army up into some semblance of marching order. Keeping the left flank to the river Kennet they moved off past Newbury and through Greenham Common and Brimpton. With them were 600 Royalist prisoners taken in the fighting.

Not all the Royalists had been happy with the decision to return to Oxford or would agree to do so prominent among these were Rupert and his cavalry officers. His grim warlike humour is reflected in a pun he made at the Council, 'although the Roundheads were marching unto Reading they would make calves of them before they came unto Veale.' (Theale).

Between Aldermaston and Padworth the Prince tried to make good his threat. Musketeers and dragoons lined the hedges in ambush. Supported by cavalry they poured fire into the Roundhead column. Stapleton's cavalry that had bourne the brunt of the fighting at Aldbourne and fought themselves to a standstill at Newbury, panicked and broke at last. Their mounts crashed through the packed infantry in the steep sided lanes. Infantry under the command of Colonel Middleton took to the hedges and ditches and returned the Cavalry fire. After heavy casualties the Royalists were forced to withdraw for lack of men to sustain

the attack. Once more the Parliament army was able to move off but not before the guards turned on their prisoners in outrage, 'they knocked out their brains with the butt end of their muskets.'

All that remained was the march through the safe countryside of the Thames Valley. Through Reading, Maidenhead and Windsor the tired soldiers returned to a triumphant entry into London. Probably the greatest military march ever undertaken through England was safely over. There were hundreds of dead to prove it.

CHAPTER SEVEN

BERKSHIRE - SPRING AND SUMMER 1644

In April 1644 the Committee of Both Kingdoms, sitting at Derby House in London, were attempting to co-ordinate several armies in the field. They were also trying to contend with the personal animosities of the commanding generals. The fact that the same commanders were also members of the Committee did nothing to smooth the situation. Each officer had success to his credit, the most recent being Waller's victory at Cheriton (29 March).

An encounter shortly after Cheriton fight reveals that not all courteous behaviour had been blunted by war. Lady Hopton, wife of Sir Ralph, was captured near Newbury. Her two coaches, twelve coach horses and escort were apprehended. Orders were given that she should be treated with the respect due to a lady of quality and she and her attendants were allowed to keep their personal jewellery. Lady Hopton was allowed to continue her journey to Oxford. (1)

Some of the exchanges between the Roundhead Committee members were less courteous. The principle complication being the individual members opinions as to the political future of any final victory over the King.

Before any final victory could be achieved the majority agreed that Oxford would have to be taken. To this end, the Earl of Manchester and Essex were instructed to rendezvous at Aylesbury by 19 April. Manchester was to lead his army of the Eastern Association and Essex would have his strength reinforced by City of London levies. This would leave Waller free to move west and engage Prince Maurice.

The outcome was, Manchester refused to move, fearing the advance of Prince Rupert into the counties of his association, Waller's City regiments demanded they be allowed to return home and Essex petulantly wrote to the committee, '... you have been pleased to reduce my army by 7000 foot and 3000 horse, when my Lord of Manchester is allowed an army of 14,000 and received 34,000 a month for the pay of it.' (2)

The Royalist Council of War, meeting at Oxford, was certainly more unified as to the political future intended should they gain victory. But personal conflicts still contributed greatly to the undoing of well laid military plans.

Eighteen months occupying the Oxford area had revealed that in order to maintain such a large army in the area control of the surrounding counties was essential. A Royal Proclamation issued at Oxford on 15 April 1644 was addressed to 'Our Loving Subjects of Oxford and Berkshire'. The content of the Proclamation shows they had not been, or probably been able, to be as loving as the King would have them. They were sternly admonished over the small amounts of corn, hay and straw being brought into Oxford for the armies use. They were warned that should they fail to increase the quota by any pretext whatsoever, the soldiers would be sent to collect their needs and burn what was left, rather than see it fall into the hands of the rebels. (3)

To protect Oxford, and to add to the burden of the inhabitants who had to supply them, a number of garrisons were placed in fortified towns and private houses. Reading was refortified when the Royalists again occupied the county town. Wallingford, Abingdon, and Faringdon were strengthened and Donnington was strongly held. Rupert's voice in council called for these places to be maintained while a strong body of cavalry should be kept at Oxford to reinforce any of them should the need arise. Their very existence would deter a march on Oxford, he argued.

In early April the King decided to take stock of his army by holding a review of the regiments. Regiments were instructed to move out from Oxford, Bristol, Malmesbury and the Forest of Dean, and rendezvous at Marlborough. There the King would, 'by his presence' give them encouragement.

Tuesday 9 April, the King left Oxford with his troop of horse, their captain, Lord Bernard Stuart. That evening the King reached Childrey, near Wantage, where he spent the night at Lady Fettyplace's Rampaynes Manor. Lord Bernard lodged at Wilmot's house and the troop quartered in Wantage. The army was joined at Wantage by some regiments of horse that had been waiting the rendezvous at Blewbury.

The following morning the King and his escort reached Aldbourne and on the Chase the whole army paraded for inspection. There were fifteen regiments of foot, a total of 5000 men, seventy ensigns led them, the square colours flying. Four brigades of horse, made up of twentysix small regiments added their panoply to the scene.

Later, a Council of War was held in Marlborough, presided over by the King. It was agreed the army was ready to embark on the summer campaign and Sir William Waller, nicknamed 'William the Conqueror', was the opponent selected. After the meeting the King retired for the night to the home of Lord Seymour in the town.

On returning to Oxford the following day, he declared a recess of the Oxford Parliament. The Queen was now expecting her eighth child and the King deemed it safer she should leave Oxford for the west country. On Wednesday, 17 April, in the afternoon, the King escorted his wife and the two princes to Abingdon, the first stage of her journey. There, while they said their goodbyes, Richard Symonds of the King's Troop made yet another entry in his Diary of the Civil War Marches. 'As we marched in Abingdon I saw a tall stout fellow, whose hair was all matted in elf-locks, very long, and his beard so too, though not so large. His nose cutt or eate off.'(4) King and Queen parted, the King returned to Oxford and the Queen towards Lambourn, the next leg of her journey. She was to have many adventures before reaching the safety of the continent; they were never to see each other again.

After Aldbourne the army moved to Newbury where they quartered in and around the town. On 16 April Parliament associated Berkshire with Hampshire and Wiltshire, an association which did not last and later the county was more logically associated with Bucks' and Oxon. This device of association between

Seal of the Commonwealth.

counties was designed as a mutual protection and recruitment catchment area. Such are the materials of civil war that at the same time as Parliament were associating Berkshire in their interest, Colonel Richard Neville, High Sheriff of the county, was recruiting a regiment of auxiliaries in Reading for the King. The Reading regiment never saw action, they were disbanded a few weeks later.

On the same day as the Ordinance was passed a party of Roundhead horse from Winchester beat up Royalist quarters at Sonning. A number of officers and men were either killed or captured and forty much needed horses were taken back into Hampshire. (5)

News reached the King in May that both armies of Essex and Waller had been reinforced. The Earl of Essex arrived in Windsor with his army and instructions were sent informing the Windsor Regiment to march with the Earl - when he left. This they refused to do unless they were paid first, the pay for the garrison, leaving out horse and artillery, came to £3000 a month and was well in arrears. Venn was given a free hand to raise money by assessments, twentieth parts and sequestrations. He raised over £300 in Windsor town alone. It was intended to denude Windsor of troops, the minister, surgeons, quartermaster, marshall and commissary were ordered to accompany the Windsor regiment when it left. Berkshire militia were ordered to take up garrison duties in the castle once Essex was ready to march. While the Earl mustered and trained his forces at Windsor, Waller prepared his at Farnham.

At the Marlborough Council of War, Lord Forth had found almost complete support for his plan to once again abandon Reading, this time voluntarily. This would increase the strength of the Oxford army by some 3000 men. Knowing Rupert was opposed to such a plan, the King tried to delay the move being put into effect. The moving of the army from Marlborough to Newbury enabled a watch to be kept on Reading, Wallingford and Oxford, should Parliament make their move.

The King's advisers at Oxford were not certain whether Essex intended a march directly on Oxford or if he would use the same tactics as before and make Reading the first stop. Reading was warned by Edward Nicholas, the King's Secretary, on April 20 that 3000 men were marching from London, their design being Reading. The commander of the garrison was instructed to discover which parties in the town were affected to the rebel cause. Nicholas further instructed Forth to send scouts into eastern Berkshire to discover Essex's approach march. Forth requested he should move his army nearer to Reading and the King agreed to a leaguer or camp being set up between Wallingford and Reading. Forth moved to Childrey and from there he found he could direct his forces and keep close contact with Oxford. On 10 May a Council of War was called at Abingdon and Forth, Astley, Hopton, Wilmot attended, the King presided. It was decided to go ahead with the destruction of the Reading defences and the town to be abandoned.

The slighting began immediately and all the Berkshire villages under Royalist control were ordered to send in men, spades, picks and shovels to speed up the work of reducing the defences. Within five days the work was well in hand, guns, twenty barrels of powder and match were sent by barge and cart to

Wallingford. Four cannon, ten barrels of powder, match and bullet were delivered to Donnington Castle, the rest of the magazine was placed into Oxford.

Forth had been granted a warrant to impress men in Berkshire. They were to strengthen his regiment and two officers were sent to Abingdon to collect the men. Of the 334 impressed only 213 were still held in the town. No sooner they moved off another 51 got away, claiming later they had not been paid. The officers returned to Reading empty handed and the Berkshire Commissioners told them to return a few days later. (6) On their hopeful return not a man was to be found.

On 16 May Charles arrived in Reading to study the progress of the work. He stayed at Coley House, south west of the town. Coley House had belonged to Sir Thomas Vachell, his widow Letitia Knollys had married John Hampden. Much of the Parliamentary opposition party was linked in this fashion, by marriage.

Charles led his army out of the slighted works of Reading on Saturday, 18 May. As they marched away towards Englefield, Colonel Hawkins led his 200 white-coated musketeers in the opposite direction, towards Henley. Their destination was the fortified Greenland House which dominated the river Thames downstream from Henley.

The 3000 men of the Reading army marched through Englefield and Bradfield, crossed the Berkshire downs and mustered at Compton Down. At Compton they met with other regiments which had been stationed away from the county town. Symonds entered in his diary, 'Here, on top of the playne hills, was the rendesvouz of the whole army that Satterday. '

The King continued on to Oxford and the army slowly made its way towards Wantage. Inactive while their enemy lay not many miles away, the horse eventually quartered into Faringdon and the foot into Abingdon. The inactivity of the Cavalier army was noted by Edward Walker, the King's Secretary-at-war:

'About the 24th of May the Foot were drawn into Abingdon, and the horse quartered at Farringdon, who (guided by I know not

64

what Fate or Disposition) had not in all this time of the Rebels advance (neither before or after the quitting of Reading) either beaten up any of the Rebels Quarters, given them any Allarms, or so much as faced them, which no question gave them great encouragement'. (7)

As the Royalists left Reading, William Waller arrived at Bagshot from Farnham. Here he greeted his reinforcements, the City Brigade and the Kentish Regiment. Serving with the Tower Hamlets Auxiliaries was a foot soldier called Richard Coe. His 'Exact Dyarie....' published shortly after the campaign paints a serving soldier's picture of the following weeks.

Essex, meanwhile, had reached Henley and his men set about constructing a bridge over the Thames for their crossing. That weekend Waller rode from Bagshot to Henley to confer with his fellow commander of the Parliament army engaged on the reduction of Oxford. It was well known that the two perfectly hated each other and were therefore far from ideal partners for such a joint venture. Waller returned to Bagshot in pouring rain, after, it can be assumed, they had reached agreement on their plan for the encirclement of the Royal stronghold.

The Earl of Essex acquainted by scouts that Reading had been abandoned, sent forward an advance occupying force. The bridge at Henley completed, Caversham Bridge repaired from the slighting, Essex led his army into Reading on 23 May. A year had passed and once again the Earl was at Reading and the King safe at Oxford.

Essex did not remain at Reading for long, continuing his march he reached Bradfield. Expecting opposition but finding none, he pressed on to Blewbury. As the Royalists went into quarters at Abingdon and Faringdon, the Roundheads encamped in the open fields between Blewbury and East Hagbourne. Wet and tired, the soldiers clustered under hedgerows, sheltering from the persistent downpour.

The following day, Saturday 25 May, a party of

Roundhead scouts were sent to probe towards Abingdon. Shortly before dusk they cautiously approached the riverside town; to their surprise it too had been abandoned.

The Royalist decision to relinquish Abingdon had been a practical one. A single regiment, augmented by the foot from Reading, held the town. Lord Forth is considered to be the leading advocate for such a course of action although there are strong grounds for believing Lord Wilmot influenced the decision. Wilmot's animosity towards Rupert and his often faulty judgement, which the King must bear the responsibility of following, went some way in affecting the outcome of the war in Parliament's favour. Later the King confessed to being 'much troubled' by the loss of Abingdon and he admitted in a letter to Rupert, 'I confess the best to have been, to have followed your advice.' The Council of War, held at Abingdon, had left the actual decision of abandoning the town open. It was to depend on the enemies line of march should they advance from Wantage or Faringdon they were to retire to Oxford.

On his return to Bagshot, Waller led his army first to Basing and then to Basingstoke. By mid-week he was ready to move north into Berkshire to affect a juncture with the Earl of Essex. One or two nights were spent in fields about Aldermaston and the Saturday night they arrived at Compton. Coe described the place, 'Compton a durty town, but we had good respects for our money..' On being told on Sunday morning that Essex had occupied Abingdon, there was 'much joy and shouting from the soldiers', Coe records. Waller marched on to Marcham where his men camped in and around the village, Abingdon already being filled with Essex's troops. Essex himself was lodging at the home of Lady Powell. Sir Edward Walker, the King's Secretary-at-war, dolefully wrote, 'and now the Rebells thought their game sure, having without a blow gott possession of Reading, Abingdon, & so all of Berkshire... '

Walker was not wholly correct, Wallingford, Faringdon and Donnington were still Royalist strongholds, but the surrounding vital countryside was certainly in rebel hands.

One of Essex's first acts on arriving in Abingdon was to issue an order against plundering, on pain of 'death without mercy'. He publicly declared that the county had already been much afflicted and he charged his officers, 'not withstanding any pretence whatsoever, to plunder or spoil any of the goods of the inhabitants.... or offer any violence.' (8)

On Tuesday, 28 May the Earl advanced his army across the Thames at Sandford Ferry. Skirting Oxford he established his head-quarters at Islip. Attempts at crossing the Cherwell were not so successful; twice they failed at Gosford Bridge and again at Enslow Bridge and Tackley Ford.

As Essex marched out of Abingdon, Waller marched in. Some of his men took up the quarters vacated by the outgoing troops and others continued through the town to Nuneham Woods where they made camp. In Abingdon Coe saw that Essex had been true to his word, two men were hanging in the market square. Pinned to their chests were notices, 'Hanged for violence and plundering'. On arrival at Nuneham Woods, fires were soon burning as the men tried to dry out their saturated clothing. In Coe's estimation they burnt £50 worth of wood in the attempt.

With Essex concentrating his forces to the east of Oxford, it was planned that Waller should cover the west. This would prevent the King escaping to the safety of Worcester.

While the Roundheads made their ineffectual attempt at crossing Gosford Bridge, a large party of Royalist troops doubled back through Oxford and out towards Abingdon. Their aim was either to retake the town or engage Waller in isolation from Essex.

Waller had divided his own forces by placing some at Nuneham and the remainder in Abingdon. The Royalist Earl of Cleveland felt confident enough to lead 150 horse against the 1000 foot and 400 horse billeted in the town. They managed to penetrate the town and after fierce street fighting the sheer weight of numbers forced them to withdraw to Oxford. Captains de Lyne and Trist of Prince Charles' Regiment were slain in the withdrawal. Later

the King's troop brushed with Roundheads at Cumnor, inflicting a number of casualties.

To affect his design of circling Oxford to the west, Waller had first to cross the Thames. The nearest point for such a crossing was at Newbridge and after camping overnight in Appleton Woods his forces made an attempt on the bridge. Parts of the structure had been destroyed and a Royalist unit of dragoons guarded both banks. According to the Royalist paper Mercurius Aulicis, the rebels were driven back 'both with shame and loss'. The writer further claimed that Waller was so vexed by the failure that he revenged himself 'upon Abingdon Cross ... which they so manfully assaulted and pulled down to the ground.' The 'Cross on the Bury' dated from 1441 and this, church windows, chancel screen and other objects offensive to Puritan eyes were wantonly destroyed. Houses were looted on the pretext that the owners were Royalists and churches and chapels were turned into stables.

On Saturday I June, Waller ordered a concentrated effort to be made on securing the bridge. Two files were drawn out from each company as a Forlorn Hope, or front line. Led by Captain Gore of the Tower Hamlets Regiment and a captain from the Kentish Regiment, they drew the defenders fire. The musketeers guarding the bridge had retired to the Oxford bank where they had prepared earthwork defences. While the forlorn hope engaged the defenders, a larger party of Roundheads crossed the river downstream. First they had ferried across the river in punts, then using the punts as floating arches, planks were laid across to form a bridge. Taken by complete surprise the Royalists continued fighting until it became clear they were not only hopelessly outnumbered but any chance of relief was effectively cut off by the force that had crossed the river. They were finally forced to surrender when powder and ball ran out, the few survivors were taken prisoner and escorted back to Abingdon.

The following afternoon after Roundhead pioneers had laboured to repair and to strengthen the bridge, Waller's regiments arrived on the Oxford side. (9) A number of captive Irish women, camp followers of those taken the day before, were 'whipt and turned away' to fend for themselves.

The King now faced the prospect of being completely surrounded and trapped in Oxford within days. With Waller across the Thames it could not be long before Essex forced the Cherwell crossings. After a Council of War, the Royalists planned a daring attempt at slipping between the two converging armies under cover of darkness. The bulk of the army would go with the King and it was hoped the Roundheads would follow rather than lay siege to an empty town. As a cover to the army's movement, over 3000 foot and a small train of artillery feinted towards Abingdon. Waller, fearing that this was a real attempt to regain the town and cut him off, was forced to return over Newbridge to guard his base. While he was occupied in this fashion, Essex prepared to cross the Cherwell the following day. The King made his move, between nine and eleven at night of 3 June, the Royalists quietly left Oxford towards the Witney and Burford road. Within three days, after the fastest march of the war, they were safe at Worcester.

On the morning of 6 June, William Waller and the Earl of Essex, in company with their senior officers, met, probably at Chipping Norton. At this meeting the most extraordinary decision was taken despite some opposition. Waller would continue his pursuit of the King while Essex would detach his forces and march west to the relief of Lyme Regis. London was notified, and probably expecting their reaction, Essex quickly set out. The next day he was at Burford, on the 8th Faringdon and on the 10th Lambourn. By the time the Committee, sitting at Derby House, could order him back, he had reached Blandford. He refused and carried on to meet disaster in Cornwall. Coe, still with Waller chasing the King's army, complained, 'it rained extremely as it had done for the most part since the advance. ' If Oxford's capture had been the objective, he and his fellow soldiers had got wet for nothing.

CHAPTER EIGHT

ABINGDON - SUMMER 1644

The ease with which. their armies had plucked Reading and Abingdon from the Royalists, came as something of a surprise to Parliament. In particular their good fortune in acquiring Abingdon, a base so close to Oxford.

Occupying, retaining and maintaining the two Berkshire towns however presented them with a number of problems. The Parliament armies were fully committed and the condition of the reserves was poor. Pay and supplies were often weeks behind and already differences over religion and politics were beginning to surface. Whoever was appointed to command the garrison at Abingdon would have to bear the brunt of complaints from discontented, often hungry and unpaid soldiers, coupled with the bitter emnity of the country people. Parliament's choice fell upon Major General Richard Browne.

Contemptuously known to Royalists tractarians as 'Major General Wood-Monger', he was at it suggests a wood merchant in civilian life. A Londoner, he commanded the London Trained Band regiments, the White and Yellow, under Waller at Cheriton. (1) Like Waller, Browne was a Presbytarian but there was little love lost between the two, Waller having already blocked Browne's promotion. Browne was described in one pamphlet as 'a man of clear courage and good under standing and very crafty'. As events in Abingdon were to show, the latter was more than true.

On 8 June, 1644, Parliament appointed, by ordinance, Major General Browne, commander of those forces raised by Parliament for 'reducing Oxford, the Town and Castle of Wallingford, the fort of Greenland House and the Town and Castle of Banbury'. (2) His commission also gave him control of those forces raised in the counties of Berks, Bucks' and Oxon'. The same month Parliament strengthened their control over Berkshire with a clearly defined ordinance.

'June 27th 1644. For the Better Execution of the Orders and Ordinances of Parliament in the Severall Counties of Berkshire,

Buckinghamshire and Oxon and for the Raising of Money and Forces within the said counties; for Suppressing the Rebels there and for the Maintenance of all such Garrisons within the said Counties, as are or shall be Erected by Authority of Parliament for the Better Defence of the Same.
1. For Voluntary loans and Contributions to Parliament.
2. For collecting weekly Assessments.
3. For collecting the impasts known as the Fifth and Twentieth Rart.
4. For the Sequestration of Papists' and Delinquents Estates.

The county was judged able to be assessed, taxed and levied up to the sum of £400 a week. The committees were also given authority to take 'Sufficient Timber' which stood on the land owned by 'Papists or Delinquents'. They were also empowered to call before them 'all Ministers, and School-masters that are scandalous in their lives or ill-affected to the Parliament, or that have deserted their Cures, or ordinary places of residence, not having sufficient ground for their absence'. (3) Nearly forty Berkshire Royalists compounded for their estates which were sequestered by Parliament. A number of prominent people were reported as being Papists, including Gabriel Coxe, Mayor of Newbury. (4)

County men, sympathetic to Parliament, were appointed committee members to implement the conditions laid down in the ordinance. The members were the Speaker of the House, William Lenthall, Sir Francis Knollys, Sir Francis Pile, Robert Pye, the elder, Sir Benjamin Rudyard, Richard Whitehead, Edmund Dunch, Henry Marten, Peregrine Hoby, Tanfield Vachell, Daniel Blagrave, William Ball, John Packer the elder and Robert Packer, and Cornelius Holland. Major General Browne was also appointed, probably to help ensure the members were diligent in their offices. Some needed no encouragement.

Three regiments of Auxiliaries were placed under Browne's command. The Red commanded by Colonel Harsnet, the Blue by Colonel Pinder and the White under Colonel Shepherd. 4000 strong, they marched out of

London on Thursday 20 June. Too late to be of assistance to Waller at Cropredy Bridge, (29 June) when the King, after a long march, had turned on him and soundly defeated his army, the two Roundhead officers met at Towcester. While at Northampton, Browne's troops mutinied. The General managed to quell the outbreak but was wounded in the face during a fracas. Leaving Waller to operate in Northamptonshire and Bucks, Browne marched his regiments to lay siege to Greenland House.

Some of the Earl of Essex's soldiers had already suffered a smart rebuff at the hands of Colonel Hawkins and his musketeers. The Roundheads had been out to 'view the works' of Greenland House and when driven off had been taunted with the suggestion that the Earl should call again if passing. In high tone, Essex replied, 'he would not only call, but Knocke'. Recommendations as to the best way of reducing Greenland House had already been put forward. It had been suggested that Browne would be the most suitable commander to undertake the siege. He was advised Greenland House could be battered in three places, demi-cannon and culverins being advocated. A barge containing cannon could be fired from the river and, it was added, seamen would be the best suitable to affect such an attack. (5)

When, after Cropredy the King elected to take his army in pursuit of Essex, the Lords at Oxford sought ways in which to support Greenland. Its position, dominating the river, hindered the river traffic and in particular hampered the barges carrying vast amounts of wood removed from 'malignants' estates in Berkshire. On Monday, 8 July, Colonel Thomas Lunsford, with troops from Wallingford and Oxford, placed two months supply of provisions into Greenland.

The day following Lunsford's arrival, Browne drew up his regiments before the outworks. The recommended guns were placed into position supported by mortar. After three days of fire, a grenade hit the powder magazine in the house. Hawkins and his Whitecoats surrendered to honourable terms.

Greenland House was surrendered on 12 July, the same day Parliament passed an Ordinance for the three counties to raise forces for Browne's use, it was hoped to raise 1000 foot, 200 horse and 200 dragoons. A few days later the committee for Berkshire was empowered to press 500 soldiers for the use of Parliament.

The need for extra men was evident when Browne arrived in Reading on Wednesday 17 July. He had his London regiments, a weak Windsor unit and the Hertfordshire Trained Bands. Many had deserted either from want of pay, poor clothing or simply wishing to return home for the harvest or business.

By Sunday the Major General was able to give a report on the poor defence of the town and he recommended Harrison's Barn be fortified and two new forts be built to command the entrances to Reading. By this he estimated Reading could be protected by between 1000 and 1500 men. A force this small, in his consideration, would not prevent the Royalists plundering the town but it would effectively prevent them occupying it again. His Hertfordshire men were now actively petitioning to return home and eventually this was permitted. (6)

On Monday Browne was ordered to Abingdon where two days previously, Waller had arrived with the Train of Artillery. Waller had been instructed to try and stop the Royalists of Wallingford garrison plundering the surrounding countryside. On being informed he would be expected to take orders from Waller, Browne was quick to point out that he now possessed an independent command. As Major General of the three counties he would only take orders from the Earl of Essex who was Lord General, the Committee of Both Kingdoms and Parliament.

Browne's soldiers refused to leave Reading until they had been paid and the Committee for the Associated Counties advanced enough money for Browne to get the army on the move by Saturday. They arrived at Blewbury the following day only to be ordered back into Reading.

Harrington's City Brigade, serving under Waller, were requested to remain at Abingdon until they could be replaced. Derby House were worried about the safety of the town and were apprehensive should they lose something they had so easily gained. William Ball, M.P. for Abingdon and member of the Berks' committee (while in Parliament he served on some 34 committees), was urged to do all in his power to persuade Harrington's and Waller's soldiers to remain with their regiments. At the same time Derby House requested the Kent committee to spare horse, dragoons and a foot regiment to go to Abingdon.

Browne was still in Reading when £1000 arrived from London, via Windsor, to pay the Abingdon forces. Arrangements were made with the Berks' committee for the money to be escorted to Abingdon by captains' Grenville and Tyrrell. (7) Browne had received word that 500 Royalist horse had arrived at Wallingford. This sudden influx of fresh troops in the area seriously worried Browne. A force this strong could, if it so desired, raid as far from Wallingford as Newbury where Major Temple and Captain Askew with their troops of horse were stationed with a small number of foot. Already Abingdon was reporting its quarters were being beaten up by Royalists from Wallingford and Abingdon and although each attack had been beaten off the threat was ever present.

Browne was next instructed to move into Buckinghamshire, he reached Henley and was diverted again. On Wednesday, 14 August, Major General Browne finally arrived in Abingdon.

The town was so crowded when Browne's forces arrived, they were forced to bed 10 to a room. As he approached the town he noted the surrounding countryside was being 'despoiled and ruined by the soldiers'. (8) On arrival the Warwickshire Trained Bands were allowed home for the harvest and Browne gave them Colonel Vandrusque's horse as escort, 'the rather I might be freed from the hourly complaints of the poor country about, ruined by the soldiers', he wrote. Derby House notified Browne that reinforcements were on their way and ordered Waller to leave Abingdon on 26 August, with his Train of Artillery, for Hampshire.

Waller left instead for London to get his voice heard but the train was forced to stay for lack of horses. The following day Colonel Ayloffe and Lieutenant Colonel Sadler arrived with 600 horse.

That very day the quarters were beaten up again by Cavaliers from Wallingford. Within three days of the reinforcements arriving over 100 had deserted. With no pay in their pockets they had sold their bread and cheese ration to the local people to raise funds to get them home. Browne was left with two operational troops of horse to guard the approaches to the town and protect any supplies being brought in.

Mr Gunton, an engineer, was charged with constructing Abingdon's defences. Browne utilised the artillery left by Waller but when Derby House heard of this they urged him in no way to delay its departure. The Berks' committee was instructed to supply Colonel Holborne with carts and transport to remove the heavy guns and ammunition Venn, at Windsor, was ordered to move guns down river to Reading from where they would be moved to Abingdon. Still Browne failed to comply, excusing the delay by claiming there were no horses available as they were being used in the harvest. In mitigation he said he had at least managed to obtain 13 carts. Wallingford, well aware of Browne's predicament, were busily sweeping up as many draught horses as they could lay their hands on.

Forces, withdrawn from the siege of Donnington, were ordered to march to Abingdon. Aware of the conditions in the town they deserted by the dozen on the journey, making it clear they were not going 'there to starve'.

In September, when the Cavalier Colonel Gage relieved Basing House in his daring ride, Browne was powerless to stop him. Gage had timed his movements well, Waller's carts were at last on the road and had to be withdrawn. The Roundheads had no real idea of Gage's target and to confuse them Gage had sent a decoy party to the Faringdon side of town to draw out their hard pressed horse. Major Underwood set out with 150 musketeers on borrowed horses but ended up fruitlessly patrolling the Newbury area. Later Browne confessed to being 'shamed, over the handling of the whole affair'.

CHAPTER NINE

THE RELIEF OF BASING HOUSE - SEPTEMBER 1644

The catalogue of Parliamentary successes in the Berkshire area presented a grim picture to the Royalist Council of War sitting at Oxford in the King's absence. Reading and Abingdon abandoned, Greenland House surrendered, Donnington under almost constant siege and Faringdons defences found to be dangerously poor in the event of an attack. Forty miles to the south, Basing House, beset now for three months and within days of having to 'submit to the worst conditions the rebels are like to grant to my person and religion', according to its defender John Paulet, Fifth Marquess of Winchester.

The Council were not unmindful of the pressure on Basing House, ringed as it was by the combined Parliament forces of Hampshire and Sussex under the command of Colonel Richard Norton. Any doubts they may have held were soon dispelled by the personal plea of the Marchioness who had made the hazardous journey to Oxford to lobby the members.

It was Colonel Henry Gage, a veteran of the Continental wars, who offered his services to the council to affect a relief; much to the dislike of the Oxford Governor, Sir Arthur Aston, (last seen nursing a sore head leaving Reading). Gage, a Roman Catholic, as were Paulet and the majority of the Basing defenders, was mindful of the fact that 'the service full of hazard', held most of its danger in the return journey. Browne lay at Abingdon conveying the false impression he had sufficient horse to control the area, Reading and Newbury held large numbers of dragoons; these would all be alerted once Basing was relieved.

Gage's force was hastily made up from volunteers. Lords and gentlemen were encouraged to give up their own horses to servants willing to go. Colonel Hawkins, late of Greenland House, pledged his whitecoat musketeers. A body of horse under Sir William Campion, Governor of Boarstall House, swelled the numbers. According to Gage, 'With somewhat more than 400 musketeers of Her Majesty's and Colonel Hawkin's Regiment, and 250 horse of My Lord Treasurer's Regiment, commanded by

Colonel Webb of Sir Arthur Aston's Regiment ... ' he was ready to make the attempt'. Lieutenant-Colonel Buncle and the ill-fated Major Windebank, completed Gage's staff. The strong Catholic influence within the Royalist party was seldom more evident than now when a stronghold of their religion was threatened with annihalation.

On Monday 9 September, at about ten at night the party left Oxford. Diversionary horse had been sent towards Abingdon and the whole force wore orange-tawny scarves in the hope of deceiving enemy scouts that might see them. Later the Parliament tractarians exaggerated the number of Cavaliers to 1400 horse and foot, it was probably only half that number. Marching all night, passing not more than two miles from Abingdon, they reached the shelter of Cholsey Woods, near Wallingford, next morning. They had covered fourteen miles without discovery.

During the three hour rest allowed by Colonel Gage, they were reinforced by Captain Walters with 50 foot and 50 horse from Wallingford Castle. A messenger was sent ahead to Winchester with Gage's instructions to Sir William Ogle's force for a diversion in the enemy's rear. They were to attack, 100 horse and 300 foot strong, through Basing Park. The garrison would make sallies from the house and Gage would fall on from the Berkshire side. The combined attack was timed to occur between four and five o'clock the next morning. The messenger safely on his way, the men rested and reinforced, Gage led them off again through the by-lanes towards Aldermaston.

To maintain a fast pace through the hostile county Gage had the foot ride behind the troopers and even change places at intervals. Setting an example he allowed a musketeer to ride his horse while he walked alongside for three miles. Captain Walters with his troop of horse were sent ahead with the quartermasters to prepare Aldermaston village as the next resting place.

Arriving in the village Walters surprised a troop of Roundhead horse allegedly burning prayer books and cutting up a surplice. Forgetting the cover of their orange scarves and the white ribbons in their hats, they attacked. One Roundhead was killed and six captured but others escaped towards Reading and Basing.

At eight o'clock Gage arrived in Aldermaston with the main party and was made aware of the fresh situation. His men, weary from lack of sleep, a days forced march and the constant tension of being in enemy country, had to have some rest. Gage could only allow them until one in the morning. Reading, only nine miles away, was slow to react, but not Colonel Norton laying siege to Basing House.

John Paulet at Basing House was also soon aware of the Aldermaston incident. Not knowing how this would affect Gage's plan and faced with a rising mist, all he could do was order a great fire to be lit above the Gatehouse to guide the relief force should it still come.

By now Gage was beginning to lose men suffering from exhaustion and he passed among them promising plunder when they reached Basing or reward when they returned to Oxford. Arriving at Chineham Down, two miles from Basing, the Cavaliers discovered the enemy under Norton in strong positions. The hedges had been lined with musketeers and on the hillside stood 'a body of five cornets of horse, very full, standing in good order.' Worse still, Lieutenant Swainley, sent by Ogle from Winchester, informed Gage that no support could be expected from that quarter. Major Ludlow, with a strong rebel force, lay between Winchester and Basing, blocking off the Park.

Gage called a Council of War to acquaint his officers with the situation. No longer was there the element of surprise, no support to draw off the enemy, tired troops facing fresh opposition and the Roundheads already in chosen battle positions. After deliberation the council meeting ended with the decision to 'fall on jointly and at one place.'

Colonel Webb took command of the right wing, Buncle the left and Gage the centre. Gage went from unit to unit offering encouragement and ordering the men to tie a white ribbon or handkerchief above the right elbow. Further identification in the melee and fog would be the password 'St George'. A messenger was sent to make an attempt at getting into Basing House to inform Paulet of these details and request him to send forth diversionary sallies once the engagement comenced. With all preparations made, the fog lifting as daylight broke, Colonel Gage led the way, on foot, sword drawn.

The Cavalier advance was met by a hail of musket fire from the hedges, 'more terrible than damageable'. Both wings of Gage's horse charged which, probably from its sheer desperation, forced the men lining the hedges to retreat. The foot met with tougher resistance but the Whitecoats and the Queen's Life Guard pressed forward gaining ground. Each hedge and ditch was hotly contested as the Cavaliers advanced. The sound of battle with its musket fire, clash of steel and trumpet and drum, penetrated the still morning air. The besieged garrison heard it through the mist and sallied out. Now being attacked on two sides the Roundheads began to break and run for the safety of their emplacements about Basing House. The rebel horse led the way and once they saw they were to be abandoned the infantry set off after them in headlong flight from Gage and his Cavaliers. Musketeers from the house began to clear a way through the enemy lines for the relief column to enter. Basing House had been relieved.

In the cold light of day Gage, Paulet and Colonel Norton began to count the cost. Norton was wounded in the hand and one account put his dead at 120 with 100 prisoners taken, this was later reduced to 70. Two of the prisoners were shot while attempting to escape. On the Royalist side, Captain Sturges of the Life Guard and Mr Stoner, a cornet of the Wallingford troop, were dead, along with only nine others. Four Royalists had been captured, including Master Stanhope, captured while attempting to take a Roundhead colour.

The following two days were hectic ones for the Cavaliers. One hundred Whitecoats, with an equal number of musketeers from the house, attacked the siege positions. Basing Church, which had been turned into a fortification, was captured by storming. It was market day in Basing so Gage took the opportunity to go

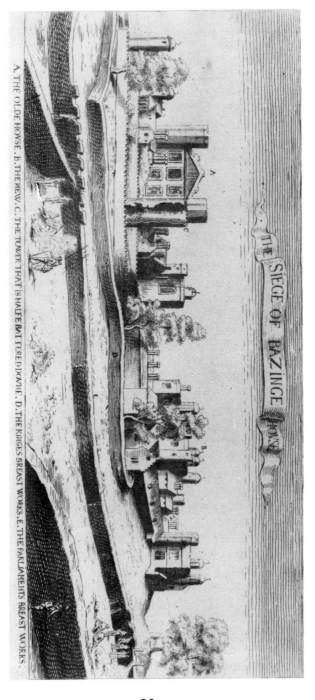

Contemporary print depicting Basing House towards the end of the first Civil War.

A. THE OLDE HOVSE . B. THE MEW. C. THE TOWER THAT IS HALFE BATTERED DOWNE . D. THE KINGES BREAST WORKS . E. THE PARLIAMENTS BREAST WORKS .

THE SIEGE OF BAZINGE HOVSE

shopping for supplies, he didn't stop to pay. A magazine was over-run and 14 barrels of powder and 100 muskets taken. Beef cattle and sheep were herded into the precincts of the houses. Temporary huts and tents, erected by the rebels along with gun emplacements, were destroyed. Large numbers of Roundheads were either killed, captured or driven off. The almost frenzied activity on the part of Gage's forces left the Roundheads shaken and almost totally unprepared for the planned return to Oxford.

Gage had warrants sent to close by towns and villages indicating they would be paid a visit the next day for the collection of supplies. By the certain capture of the warrants he hoped the enemy would be unprepared for his departure. His own scouts informed him, quite wrongly as it transpired, that 500 horse and dragoons commanded by Major General Browne waited at Aldermaston. Newbury's troopers lay at Thatcham and all the horse Reading could muster were stationed at Padworth. The main crossing points over the Kennet were thus closed to Gage. During the early evening the colonel sent parties of horse in advance once again wearing orange-tawny scarves. If stopped they were to try and pass themselves off as Norton's advance guard protecting the south side of the river.

At eleven o'clock on the Thursday night Gage led his main force from Basing House. Striking north-east and keeping wide of the Roundhead line, almost into Reading, they safely crossed the Kennet at Burghfield. The bridge had been broken down and the crossing was made with the infantry mounted on the hind-quarters of the cavalry mounts. Once across they pressed on towards the Thames and crossed the river by a ford at Pangbourne between eight and nine Friday morning. Within hours the tired and hungry soldiers were marching into Wallingford. They rested in the castle for the night and the march continued early the following day bringing the victorious Cavaliers safely into Oxford.

One account put Colonel Gage's losses at 100 killed and many captured. A number of the scouts sent ahead either fell into rebel hands or were killed in skirmishes. When Gage penned his report to the Lords at Oxford he would or could not estimate the casualties his party had inflicted but he admitted to capturing 100 Parliament soldiers. A later writer put the number killed at 120 and 150 captured. Whatever the true figure Clarendon is best left with the last word, 'it was confessed by enemies as well as friends that it was as soldierly an action as has been performed in the war on either side'.

CHAPTER TEN

THE CAMPAIGN IN THE WEST - SUMMER 1644

' I thought it fit to look after myself ....'
The Earl of Essex after deserting his army.

The fortunes of both sides took dramatic turns during the wet summer of 1644. Waller, after parting company with Essex, was defeated at Cropredy Bridge (29 June). In turn the Royalists, under Prince Rupert, were soundly beaten at Marston Moor.

The Earl of Essex had gone on to some success in the west country. Lyme was relieved, Weymouth and Melcombe Regis occupied. The Parliamentarians reaching Tavistock on 23 July had the affect of lifting the Royalists siege on Plymouth. Robert Pye, now a colonel, in company with Colonel Blake, took Taunton Dean, capturing 1 demi-culverin, 10 small guns, 2 tons of match and 8 barrels of powder.

After the engagement at Cropredy, the King's Council of War elected to follow Essex, as much as anything to protect the Queen, by now at Exeter. The army set out in pursuit on 12 July.

The Committee of both Kingdoms appreciated the danger Essex and his army could be in. Waller's forces were badly shaken, even mutinous, and it was Lieutenant-General Middleton who was sent westward. Middleton was given 2000 horse and dragoons and supplies were sent to Essex, by sea, via Plymouth.

Aware of the danger building at his rear, Essex called a Council of War. The Earl's vote was for turning and facing the approaching Royalists. In this he was opposed by many of his officers who owned large estates in Cornwall. They had rents in arrears which the hoped to collect by carrying on into the county. On 26 July Essex led his army across the River Tamar. The same day the Royalists entered Exeter. As the Roundheads moved on the King's army swiftly closed the gap

between them. Soon Essex and his army were trapped in the narrow stretch of land between Lostwithiel and Fowey.

The Cavaliers were being reinforced locally but Essex's only hope, Middleton, was pushed back in a skirmish near Bridgewater. Desperately the Parliament horse forced their way out of the trap and escaped. The Earl of Essex left by ship from Fowey, the foot under Skippon were left to surrender.

Granted so-called honourable terms, the infantry surrendered 42 cannon, a mortar and 5000 arms. Between five and six thousand soldiers were given a guarantee of safe conduct and an escort into Somerset where they were to be taken over by Middleton. Over one thousand of them either starved, died of disease or exposure, or were murdered by their fellow countrymen. Despite the instructions of the King that they were to be protected by his cavalry, they were unmercifully plundered by the Royalist infantry; many a Cavalier foot soldier remembered the withdrawal from Reading and the treatment they received at Roundhead hands.

Parliament, surprisingly perhaps, laid little blame on Essex when he returned to London. They seemed more relieved that he had escaped capture and they prepared to make Middleton the scapegoat. The immediate danger they thought was perhaps the King would now march back on London. The Earl of Manchester and Oliver Cromwell were ordered to move south in the direction of Berkshire. Waller, his army reinforced, was instructed to move west.

The King, however, had no such grand design. His aim was simply to move his army back safely into winter quarters about Oxford and at the same time to bring some relief to the three garrisons, Donnington, Basing and Banbury. He even depleted his forces by detaching men for garrison duties and quartering in the west.

Somewhat reluctantly Manchester had reached Reading and Waller had meanwhile positioned his horse at Shaftesbury.

The Earl of Essex was at Portsmouth facing the remains of his infantry. Arms and clothing were being sent down to Portsmouth to replace those lost and the Roundhead horse was being reinforced.

One major problem was the supply of fresh mounts for the cavalry and draught horses for the Train of Artillery. An Ordinance of 30 September required 1100 animals to be raised, 500 for troopers and the remainder to be draught horses. Anticipating the King's movements the counties named where the Earl would collect the horses included Berkshire. Parliament and the Derby House Committee now feared the King would turn on each of its armies and defeat them in detail.

Again they had misjudged the King's intentions, he feared the enemy would unite its three armies against him. To combat this fear Charles had instructed his nephew Rupert to go on the offensive in the hope of drawing some of the opposition away. Having issued his instructions he renewed his advance on Oxford via Newbury.

The Roundheads were indeed uniting ahead of the Royal approach. On 3 October, Manchester, writing from Reading, gave his dispositions as two regiments of foot in Newbury, 'which is more than the town can accomodate well'. The-overcrowding was due to Browne having some of his forces in the town. The rest of Manchester's foot were quartered either in Reading or the surrounding villages. Nine troops of horse were placed between Newbury and Hungerford prepared to assist either Newbury or Abingdon if threatened. A rendezvous was planned for Manchester and Essex when the latter was in a position to march north, it was to be Newbury. Cromwell and his troops were at Banbury.

Essex's Train of Artillery arrived in Reading on 12 October, the same day Browne was warned Abingdon could be the King's target and the Major General was ordered to bring in supplies from the surrounding countryside.

Two days later Cromwell arrived in Reading to meet Manchester, his horse were some miles behind quartering at Henley. By 19 October Reading town was swamped with 3000 soldiers of the City Brigade. Essex meanwhile had reached Petersfield with his forces from Portsmouth. Waller had moved to Andover and Manchester decided to carry on to Basingstoke leaving one London regiment to guard Reading.

On 20 October it fell to William Waller to notify Parliament and the Committee, 'You can now look upon our forces as joined.'

On October 22 the Royalist army reached the outskirts of Newbury. The juncture of the Roundhead forces meant that Basing could not be relieved but the forces investing Donnington were forced to withdraw. The main Royalist force encamped on Red Heath while many were billeted in Newbury. The King took the opportunity to knight John Boys for his gallant defence of Donnington Castle, the ceremony taking place on the heath. Charles then further depleted his army by sending a strong party of horse to relieve Banbury Castle. The Earl of Northampton led his own regiment reinforced by troopers from the regiments of the Earl of Brentford and Lord Wilmot. The party reached Faringdon where they surprised a force of Roundheads, capturing twentytwo and relieving the others of 'fat oxen going to Abingdon.'

The King remained at Newbury awaiting Northampton's return, reinforcements from Rupert and still holding some hope of helping Basing House. His number was further reduced by the desertion of Sir John Urry. Urry or Hurry appears to have made a habit of changing sides. He started out as a Parliamentarian serving with Hampden at Reading siege, he changed his coat three times during the war.

The Roundheads were under the impression that the King's arrival at Newbury signalled a rendezvous of his forces in the Aldermaston area and a direct threat on Reading. That night the Parliament horse were instructed to move into Aldermaston where they encamped in the park belonging to Sir Humphrey Foster, its walls and fences already broken down by past incursions of soldiers from both sides. Other troops moved into Thatcham and Bucklebury where they clashed with Royalist outposts. The foot arrived late in the evening at Swallowfield, their marching delayed by torrential rain making the narrow roads into 'foul ways.' Its armies united, Parliament was doing all it could to supply them by moving provisions down to Windsor and by barge to Reading.

The approach of the enemy forced the King to move all his forces over the Kennet and to shelter it under the protection of the guns at Donnington. The scene was set for the second battle of Newbury.

CHAPTER ELEVEN

THE SECOND BATTLE OF NEWBURY - OCTOBER 1644

'God give us peace, for God does never
prosper us in our victories to make them
clear victories.'

The Earl of Manchester

Sometime during the daylight hours of 25 October the Earl of Manchester moved his army over the River Kennet at Lodge Farm near Radworth. From the river they marched to Bucklebury Common where they had their first brush with a Royalist outpost. Attempting to obtain the advantage of Clay Hill, then known as High Dike, Prince Maurice was able at first to drive them back.

Essex led the remainder of the army to Beenham Heath. Once there the Lord General succumbed to a bad cold and he was removed to Reading in a coach lined with a feather mattress, it appears he had been ill for over a week but the marching in the wet Berkshire roads had aggravated his condition.

The Committee of both Kingdoms had been somewhat vague as to who really commanded this joint army, placing their trust in a Council of War. The Council was to be made up of the Earl of Essex, Manchester, Lord Robartes, Sir William Waller, Sir Arthur Hesilrige and Cromwell, or the greater part of them. Without the presence of the Earl of Essex the rivalries of Manchester and Waller and the dislike of Manchester by Cromwell, could flourish. Lying before Newbury and faced with a Royalist army that they outnumbered by two to one, this council of widely divergent opinions, made its battle plan.

On Saturday 26 October, the King sent for Prince Rupert to come to his assistance and drew his army into an extremely strong defensive position. To his right lay Newbury, garrisoned with part of his army, south of Newbury stood a cavalry force to prevent surprise, a mill on the Kennet was fortified and the river was his right flank. To the left ran the

River Lambourn and this was overlooked by the earthworks and cannon of Donnington Castle; the Lambourn crossings at Bagnor and Boxford were covered by cavalry outposts.

To the front lay Shaw House and the village. The ancient earthworks about the house had been strengthened and Colonels' Blagge and Lisle commanded the breastworks protected by 1000 musketeers. To the rear Prince Maurice controlled the high ground above Speen and would shortly begin digging fresh entrenchments. In the centre lay the artillery protected by the bulk of the Royalist horse. Viewed from Donnington's remaining towers the scene resembled more a siege than an imminent field engagement.

The Roundhead army had by this time occupied the elevated ground reaching from Clay Hill towards Ashmore Green and Cold Ash.

The Parliamentary Council of War that sat to decide their battle plan was presided over by the Earl of Manchester. The daring proposal agreed upon is credited to Sir William Waller. Over half the army, under Waller and to include Skippon and Cromwell, would set out on a long detouring night march. Their object to encircle the Royalist position and fall upon Maurice at Speen. Simultaneously Manchester's forces would move against Shaw Village and Shaw House; the signal to be a single cannon shot. Apart from engaging the King on two fronts it would place the Roundheads between him and provisions at Reading and between his army and Rupert's reinforcements.

Aware of the Royalist dispositions, felt out by skirmishing that day, Waller's column set out after dark. Shooting was ordered to be continued all night from Manchester's lines to keep the Cavaliers occupied. Turning away from the opposing armies, Waller marched to Hermitage then west to Chieveley. In the early hours of the morning the army stopped to rest at North Heath. Continuing south through Winterbourne they met their first opposition at the Boxford river crossing. Colonel Boys at Donnington had observed the enemy movement, probably from the lighted matches of the musketeers, he sent a party of 25 horse to harry the column in the darkness.

The Cavaliers could do little to stop Waller and he safely crossed the Lambourn and carried on to Wickham Heath. Once there he took up a position facing Speen with Cromwell's horse to his left, together they advanced on Maurice's entrenchments.

Early Sunday morning, in the light of a cold October day, Manchester sent his men down Clay Hill. They managed to cross the river by Shaw, driving back the Royalists as they advanced. Sir Bernard Astley launched a counter attack with musketeers which successfully forced the Roundheads back, many were killed either by musket fire or by drowning in the river.

Isolated fighting took place all day but at three o'clock on the afternoon of 27 October, the Roundheads forced their way into Speen. Coming under fire from Donnington Castle they pressed on until the Royalist line broke, many fleeing back into Newbury. The very guns surrendered at Lostwithiel were retaken, the men of Essex's army embracing the cannon barrels like old friends.

The Earl of Manchester, waiting, he was to claim later, for the signal gun, delayed his main assault. Finally, at four in the afternoon, he ordered two columns of troops against Shaw House. Not only were the columns driven back but the Royalists even went into a counter attack towards Clay Hill.

The King meanwhile was being driven back hard into his own centre now Speen was overrun and was himself in some personal danger. Calling on the last of his reserves the Parliamentarians were held, then pressed back. Cromwell, to Waller's left, was still only partially engaged. Had he pressed his offensive the King may well have been taken or even slain and the war ended there and then. His apologists later claimed he was under the fire of the Donnington guns and operating in poor cavalry country, neither is good enough reason for his lack of enthusiasm that day - real politic lay close to his motives.

Cromwell's delay enabled the Cavaliers to regroup their forces and go back on the offensive about Speen. Manchester still failed to make headway on the other front and only

Sᴿ WILLIAM WALLER Knight Sargeant
Maior Generall, of ye Parliamenk army, and
a member, of ye Honoble House of Commons.

C.J pinxit   1643   Rodtermondt mendit
            Pieter Stent Excudit

Sir William Waller, Major General of Parliament's army.

darkness brought a cessation to the fighting. The King fully appreciated the tremendous battle his men had fought. Far outnumbered and attacked on two fronts they had withstood the onslaught but they could by no means be certain of repeating such efforts for another day.

Guns, baggage, treasure and wounded, were placed in the hands of Colonel Sir John Boys. Leaving burning matches on the walls and hedgerows the King managed to lead his entire army through a gap no wider than 1000 metres between his enemies. With an escort of 500 troopers, the King rode hard through the night in the direction of Bath and Prince Rupert. Prince Maurice, with the remainder of the army being escorted by his cavalry, led them away through Berkshire in the direction of Wallingford.

Daybreak revealed to Manchester, Waller and the other Roundhead officers, fields of dead animals and men, but no Royal antagonists. Two or three hundred dead lay among abandoned carts and smoking fires. Many more would die for want of surgeons of which both armies were short. Mockingly, Boys greeted them with a few shots from the safety of Donnington Castle. They, in turn, retired to a Council of War to decide whether to pursue the King.

CHAPTER TWELVE

DONNINGTON CASTLE
SEPTEMBER 1643 - OCTOBER 1644

The involvement of Donnington and its castle in the Civil War dated back to 1640. The owner, John Packer, joined the opposition to the Court Party in Parliament, by refusing the King a loan. Charles promptly sequestered his property. Both John and Robert Packer were to serve Parliament on a number of Berkshire committees during the war years

Donnington Castle's value to the Royalists lay in its position dominating the western highway. Later it would serve as part of the outer ring of forts protecting Oxford.

In September 1643, the King held Court at Newbury and appointed John Boys as commander of the castle '... for the defence of this part of our County of Berks'. Boys's strength was 200 foot, 25 horse and 4 guns, along with a number of dragoons from Sir Robert Howard's regiment. As was the accepted custom of both armies, he was commissioned to draw money and supplies from the locality, in this case the parishes contained in the Hundreds of Kintbury Eagle, Faircross and Compton, over 40 parishes in all. Boys levied a weekly payment to build the outworks, the cost of which reached £1000, a very considerable sum then.

With the money and supplies such as picks, shovels, other tools and timber, Boys set about making the castle more defensible. The 'Star Fort' system, earthworks with 'arrow head' projections which held cannon and provided multiple fire angles, had been developed on the continent. Traces of these can still be seen about the walls of the castle. Either during the construction of the earthworks or later, a secret 'sally-port' was concealed in the banking, this was probably the basis for the usual 'secret tunnel' stories associated with the castle.

Boys instigated a daily market in the village and country people were invited to bring in provisions. The Cavaliers set an unusual example here by giving fair prices for goods to those willing or unafraid to trade with them. It was claimed, admittedly by a Royalist, 'England had not a better regulated garrison and better beloved of the countrye than was this of Donnington'.

As William Waller drew his forces off from an attack on Basing House on Wednesday, 8 November he was given intelligence of a valuable prize in his vicinity. Lord Saltoun, having returned from France where he had been raising money for the King, was travelling to Oxford via Newbury. Waller sent Captain Gardiner with a troop of horse to intercept Saltoun. Saltoun had landed secretly at Southampton and reached Newbury when Gardiner ambushed him. A number of Royalists were killed in the skirmish and the money, sufficient to raise two troops of horse had it reached Oxford, was taken. It was not long before Boys made it his business to regulate Parliament traffic passing Donnington. It was not, however, until the following June that the first recorded interception took place. Two waggons and six pack horses where captured on the Bath Road. Wiltshire carriers were eventually forced to pay a sum of money for each waggon left unmolested.

The same day the waggons were taken, Colonel Norton, with two troops of horse and thirty dragoons, attacked the castle outworks. They managed to kill a sentry and run off a few horses.

Colonel Middleton's forces, heavily engaged in trying to subdue Basing House, were instructed to relieve the Earl of Essex. Despite the precarious situation Essex was in, it led to the Cornish disaster, Middleton was ordered to deal with Donnington on his move west.

With 3000 horse and a number of dragoons, Middleton launched what he thought would be a surprise attack on the outbuildings of Donnington Castle. Boys, aware of the enemies approach, had concealed his musketeers in the very buildings. The Roundheads met with a hail of fire and were driven off. Colonel Middleton then decided to formerly summon the garrison which he did on Wednesday, 31 July 1644.

'Sir', wrote Middleton addressing Colonel Boys.

'I demand you to render Donnington Castle for the use of King and Parliament. If you please to entertain a present treaty you shall have honourable terms. My desire to spare blood makes me propose this. I desire your answer. JOHN MIDDLETON'

His 'desire' was granted in a style fitting the romantic Cavalier image which is all too often a false one.

'Sir. I am instructed by His Majesty's express commands, and have not yet learned to obey any other than my Sovereign. To spare blood, do as you please, but myself and those who are with me are fully resolved to venture ours in maintaining that we are intrusted with, which is the answer of JOHN BOYS'.

Middleton was not equipped with a siege train so the assault was made with hastily constructed scaling ladders. They attacked in three places simultaneously under covering fire. The losses sustained by the Roundheads in the assault were enormous and they were compelled to draw back. Boys sent the next communication. Somewhat heartlessly he wrote, 'I have many bodies of yours, which I cannot accomodate with Christian burial'. Middleton was stung to reply, 'I conceive no inherent holiness to be in any place or burial, for all earth is fit for that use'.

On the Monday, having lost nearly 300 men in the assaults, Middleton decided to continue west. Sagely he advised his superiors that Donnington should be blocked up rather than taken. The defiant little garrison was 'recommended' by Parliament to the attention of Major-General Browne with his forces from the Associated Counties of Berks', Bucks' and Oxon'.

Browne sent his adjutant-general, Jeremy Horton, with men from Windsor, Reading and Abingdon. On 29 September Horton set up batteries at the foot of the hill on the Newbury side. For the next twelve days Horton's gunners poured shot into the towers and earthworks. Three of the south towers and the curtain wall were beaten down in the bombardment.

Under the impression he had now 'humbled the governor and his garrison', Horton sent a messenger into the castle with his terms of surrender, coupled with threats, should his offer be refused.

94

'Quarter for their lives' provided the castle was given up by 10 o'clock the following Wednesday. Boys, still defiant, replied, 'Neither your new addition of forces, nor your high threatening language, shall deter me, or the rest of these honest men with me', he went on, '... and for the matter of quarter, yours may expect the like on Wednesday, or sooner if you please....'. Horton it would appear, decided not to attack and it was not until the Earl of Manchester arrived at Donnington, that the castle was threatened again. The Earl summoned Boys to surrender in early October and met with a firm but polite refusal from the governor. He determined therefore to order an assault on the earthworks, on learning of the Earl's proposition his men, 'being well informed of the resolution of those within, declined that hot service'. Manchester returned to Reading leaving Horton to continue the siege. A battery of demi-cannon, sakers and falcons was set up on the northern, Snelsmore side, of the earthworks.

Under cover of cannon fire miners and pioneers began to sap the defences. The garrison sallied out and surprised both sappers and gunners, several were killed and a large quantity of artillery equipment was carried off. Horton settled down to reduce the castle by gun fire and over '1000 great shot' was hurled at the walls, a great deal of damage was caused to the earthworks and fabric of the castle but there were few casualties.

Horton now resorted to subterfuge. His chaplain, Master Fogg, a relative to the Captain Fogg who had looted the treasury at Windsor, was central to the plot. He dictated a letter to a Mrs Fleetwood, wife of Dr Fleetwood, serving with the garrison. The letter described the defenders as 'all lost men' should they refuse Horton's summons. She begged her husband to surrender, instructed by Fogg. The letter was then 'grudgingly' allowed in to the castle. Horton had listened to the lady's 'earnest sute' but would not allow the message in until he had been 'ordered' by higher officers. Boys saw through the entire confection and ignored the letter.

On 18 October it was learned that the King was close-by with a large army. Horton was ordered

to retire to Abingdon with his men while the Windsor soldiers were sent into Newbury and the Earl of Manchester's returned to Reading.

When the King arrived on Red Heath he sent for the gallant John Boys. He thanked the colonel and his garrison for their sterling defence and knighted Boys. In a letter dated the day after Boys was knighted, Fogg wrote to the Committee at Derby House. '... we had almost brought Donnington Castle to the ground,' he claimed, it being saved only by Colonel Horton being called away. The reverend gentleman ended his letter on a Christian note, 'Truely two or three fire-balls or grenadoes shot into it should make it ours, The Lord guide the state and be with you and us all'.

CHAPTER THIRTEEN

THE THIRD BATTLE OF NEWBURY - OCTOBER 1644

The Allied Commanders held a Council of War at Speen on the morning of 28 October. Cromwell, Hesilrige, and Waller, all argued for the pursuit of the Royalist army. Reluctantly Manchester agreed and a strong cavalry force set out under the command of Cromwell and Waller. Arriving at Blewbury they were informed that the enemy had already crossed the Thames at Wallingford. Considering further pursuit hopeless without infantry support the two officers returned to Newbury. The troops of Roundhead horse were left to find quarter in and around the villages of Blewbury, the Hagbourne's, Chilton and Harwell.

At Newbury, Cromwell and Waller asked Manchester for 3000 foot, or better still, the whole army, to advance and support the cavalry. Manchester argued against such a move, citing lack of supplies and the high desertion rate. Already officers were being sent to Reading to bring back the large numbers of soldiers that had run away. Discovering the King had left supplies, cannon and treasure with Boys for safe keeping, Manchester planned yet another attempt on Donnington Castle.

The whole army drew out before Donnington Castle and Boys was summoned to deliver it to them, 'or else they would not leave one stone upon another'. Boys in his reply once again demonstrated his contempt for the rebels, for he made, 'no other reply than he was not bound to repair it; however, by God's help, keep the ground'. As dissent grew within the Parliamentarian ranks and a senior officer versed in siegecraft died, they again offered terms, this time generous ones. Boys reply to this was couched almost in terms of exasperation with an enemy that could or would not take no for an answer. According to Clarendon, 'To all these he answered, that he wondered they would not be satisfied with so many answers he had sent, and desired them to be assured that he would not go out of the castle till the King sent him order to do so'.

During these negotiations, a Roundhead, not conversant with the finer points of gentlemanly behaviour, poisoned the castle's water supply. One of his betters informed Boys of this unsporting behaviour and a safe conduct was allowed for the well to be cleaned. Once the preliminaries were over another fruitless assault was made.

On 2 November some of the much needed supplies arrived and Manchester finally agreed to advance the whole army as far as Blewbury. Cavalry troops were sent towards Faringdon and Witney. The army moved off very slowly, taking two days to reach Harwell. While the majority of the army encamped around Blewbury Manchester refused to move further without first requesting instructions from Parliament. On Tuesday, 5 November, Manchester, still not in receipt of orders, appointed a rendezvous for his army at Compton Downs for the next morning. That night Cromwell's horse spent the night on Chilton Plain and in the morning joined Manchester at Compton.

One of the cavalry patrols now reported to Manchester that the King had arrived at Burford. On leaving Newbury after the battle, the King had joined Rupert at Bath. With 3000 horse and foot they had reached Burford via Cirencester. At Burford they were further reinforced prior to entering Oxford.

Manchester's instructions arrived from London and obviously to his satisfaction they advised against any division of his forces and recommended a return to Donnington to continue the siege.

The King reviewed his army at Oxford. Rupert was promoted Lieutenant-General of all the King's armies, Sir Jacob Astley was created Baron Astley of Reading and Colonel Gage received a well deserved knighthood for his exploits at Basing House.

On Wednesday 6 November Manchester vacated Compton and in one day was back at Newbury.

It was now the King's intention to regain his Train of Artillery and other supplies from Donnington. On Thursday the Royalist army left Oxford, arriving that night at Wallingford. Parliamentary scouts reported the Royalist presence at Wallingford but

Manchester was not certain as to the King's intentions. He was relieved however to receive further supplies and news that London was doing all in its power to send more. At Windsor match and bullet was being loaded daily into long boats lined with musketeers for escort and rowed up to Reading. Carts were being prepared in Reading and escorts were waiting to bring them safely to Newbury.

On Friday the King led his forces to Ilsley Downs and he spent the night at West Ilsley Rectory. On Saturday, with Rupert's and Gerrard's cavalry taking the lead, the Royalists moved towards Donnington via Chieveley.

It is claimed that Manchester ordered Cromwell to attempt to stop Rupert's approach. Cromwell is alleged to have refused on the grounds his horse had already been hard used ' you may have their skins, but you can have no service'. An unknown troop commander did make some effort and was badly beaten for his pains, losing 15 troopers as prisoners.

By 11 a.m. Saturday, Prince Rupert's horse controlled Snelsmore Common behind the castle. Manchester had drawn his soldiers into defences and batteries between Newbury and the castle and at Shaw Village. As the main Royalist army deployed on the heath behind the Prince, no attempt was made to stop them. Soon after mid-day they moved down from the high ground. Passing within cannon range of the Roundheads, the whole army, 'marched by the castle over the river by a mill, and two fords below it, without any opposition, and thence drew into the field between Speen and Newbury'.

It must have been at about this time that the oft' quoted clash   between   Manchester   and Cromwell occurred. On being urged to fight the Earl pointed out that no matter how many times they beat the King, he was still King, if they failed once, they would hang. Cromwell is said to have retorted that, 'if this be so, why did we take up arms at first'.

Either   Cromwell's   horse   or   Essex's   own

99

The 'murderous Prince Rupert' as depicted in a contemporary Parliamentry pamphlet.

regiment made one futile attack on the Royalist position. A few cannon shots were fired and musketeers lining the hedgerows gave fire, one ball striking the hoof of the King's mount. Hoping a cold night in the field would weaken the Royalist resolve Manchester posted some of his own soldiers into the warm billets of Shaw and Newbury.

The King achieved his objective and relieved Donnington and reclaimed his supplies and artillery. The gallant Boys had been given care of the King's crown, 'worn on some high days', the Great Seal, jewels and several of the King's writings. 18 pieces of cannon of small calibre and 6 large guns with ammunition were retrieved.

At 5 o'clock the Royalists marched away with their drums beating, trumpets sounding and colours flying. They had challenged the Parliamentarians to renew battle and they had been refused. His army retired to the fields about the castle and to Winterbourne Heath, the King spent the night in Donnington Castle. On Sunday morning the King attended Divine Service in the Parish Church of Winterbourne and the whole army held a service of thanksgiving.

The Royal departure called for another Parliamentary Council of War. Some cavalry commanders elected to pursue the King and have one more attempt at his army, there is no real evidence but it is claimed Cromwell was one of them. Aware that he was being followed Rupert hid some of his cavalry in a large barn. As the army progressed towards Lambourn with the Roundheads close behind, the hidden troopers emerged, trapping the Roundheads between the two forces. Over a dozen were killed and several captured in the skirmish. That night the King spent at Kingswood, the home of Mr Garrard, near Lambourn. While his own troop stayed at Wanborough his main army spread back as far as Wantage for quarters. It must have been a sad night for the King. The last Royal guest at Kingswood had been Henrietta Maria, on her way to Exeter. Now she was in France and he no nearer to regaining his power.

On Monday, Marlborough was instructed to be ready to receive the Royalist army and on what Symonds described in his Diary as 'a miserable wett windy day', they arrived there.

Shortly after the second battle of Newbury, the Committee of Both Kingdoms had expressly ordered the allied commanders to prevent any attempt by the King of relieving Basing House. Now this was a real possibility and Manchester moved his armies from Newbury to Aldermaston where he would be better positioned.

While staying at the Bear Inn in Hungerford the King planned such a relief. After five days Gage was detached with 1000 horse. Each rider was given bags to sling over his saddle and match was wound about their waists. Gage arrived at Basing House without incident on Tuesday 19 October to find the siege had been lifted.

Manchester, plagued yet again by lack of provisions and desertion faced the prospect of the whole Royalist army moving to Basing and there offering him battle again. Prudently he decided to move his armies into winter quarters. Derby House were loath to break up the armies into quarters. They suggested Manchester remain at Newbury to which he replied, 'No, if we do I will give them leave to New Bury me'. (1) Eventually the foot went to Reading and Henley and the horse were quartered as far afield as Farnham, Wokingham, Windsor, Maidenhead and Staines.

The condition of the Roundhead mounts was now appalling. Derby House were informed, 'Many hundreds of our horses are already dead, and the living very weak'. Not only were the soldiers in dire need of fresh mounts, 500 troopers were without horses, the Berkshire countryside was in no fit state to billet them. The general officers wrote, '... nor is the condition of the people less to be pittied, they have soe little left for themselves that wee may rightly fear a famine will fall upon them'. This fear was very real, being vouched for by many observers in Berkshire.

While Gage went to Basing the King marched the army to Great Shefford where he stayed at the home of Mr Brown. Symonds relates that a soldier was to be hanged that day for the crime of plundering. Fortunately for him the rope broke and he was spared. The next day was spent at Wantage, the King sleeping at the home of Sir George Wilmot at Chariton. His troop quartered at Kingston Lisle and on Thursday they escorted the King to Faringdon where he stayed at the home of Sir Robert Pye. Symonds described it as 'a manor howse called the Place, neare the church, a fair habitacion' - a description that would not hold for long.

From Faringdon the Royal army moved to its winter quarters at Oxford. There were hopes that Abingdon would fall to them but this came to nothing, Rupert merely covering the entrances to the town as the army passed. Both sides now had the winter in which to assess their positions, for Parliament the season was not wasted.

CHAPTER FOURTEEN

ABINGDON - 1644-45

'... the old Abingdon Law, where execution preceeded tryal'.
Statesmen of Abingdon. 1702

By mid-September, 1644, Major-General Browne's situation at Abingdon was desperate. The town defences were half finished, his men were starving, barefoot, poorly clothed and deserting in droves. Two men dropped dead of starvation in the street and the cavalry openly declared they would plunder the surrounding area and shoot any officer that dared stop them. A mutiny led to Browne condemning four men to death, after drawing lots one was shot against the churchyard wall. The Berkshire Committee did little to help. Browne complained they were only too ready to support troops stationed near their own estates while Abingdon stood defenceless. When Manchester arrived in Reading he added the weight of his words to Browne's in declaring the dangerous state of Abingdon's fortifications. To give some help the Earl positioned two troops of horse between Abingdon and Wallingford.

On 15 September there began an elaborate conspiracy which bought time for Browne and reinforced the view that he was 'very crafty'. Mr Nathaniel Barnard, a distant cousin to Browne and one time preacher in London, contacted the Major-General. His letter requested safe conduct through Berkshire for two ladies and a child. He added, 'I am grieved heartily, that we are not both of one side'. Browne granted the request, notified London of the contents of the letter and forgot it. A second communication however aroused his suspicions.

Barnard was now asking for protection for the house where he was lodging near Oxford. He claimed that he had been a prisoner of war at Oxford and had been recently freed, ending cryptically, 'I have a request to propose to you, which is for my safety and your Honour'. Enquiries revealed that Barnard far from being a prisoner, was an intimate of Lord George Digby. Barnard asked permission to come into Abingdon to dine with Browne. Browne informed London and allowed the preacher to enter the town and they dined in the presence of Browne's officers. Barnard then 'desired a word or two privately'. Now Browne's suspicions were proven, 'I found my good Cozen to be but the Ecciesiasticall Duck-coy, let fly from a higher Gamester'.

As Barnard's confidence grew he let it be known that he was 'Commanded 'to let the Major-General know he had friends that will honour you'. It was not long before this developed into 'His Majesty being aware of Browne's 'Noble qualities', a remark which must have brought a smile to the 'Wood-Monger'. Browne pretended annoyance and asked Barnard to stop talking in 'riddles'.

These shadowy dealings continued throughout September and into October and Browne used the time to further strengthen the defences and to harry Parliament over the soldiers pay. His position was still desperate but with this intrigue he was obtaining valuable time. Browne had over 500 men sick in Abingdon, an increase of over 300 in one month. Clothes and shoes were in short supply and there was starvation in the town. Grenville's and Tyrrell's horse were 'making it their business to plunder and rob shamefully the country'. Desertion was still high, pay weeks in arrears but still the defences grew about the town.

Barnard had now become more open in his approach, he told Browne, 'that there is no just or reasonable thing you can propose, in which you shall not be satisfied'. He harped on how Browne had been badly treated by Waller and enlarged on the doubtful backgrounds of the Parliamentary leaders.

On 19 October 80 troopers of Major Underwood's deserted en-masse and two weeks later the Abingdon horse quarters were beaten up and Captain Ayscough and two lieutenants killed. When the Royalists returned from the relief of Donnington, Rupert sent in a trumpeter and while his cavalry covered the town approaches, the main Royalist army marched into Oxford. Rupert and Sir Marmaduke Langdale only looked threatening, Browne sent out 200 horse in four bodies but there was little skirmishing.

Rupert was aware that there was a chance Abingdon would fall without bloodshed.

On 27 November Browne received a personal letter from Digby. In return for handing over Abingdon Browne would receive 'His Majesties Commission' as governor of the town. He could have command 'of a Brigade in His Majesties Army' and a warrant to become 'a Baronet'.

Now Browne was out of his depth and he urgently asked Derby House for instructions. He was instructed to continue the deception as long as possible. On receipt of his orders from London Browne had a number of secret arrests made in the town of known agents. Digby sent the Major-General an elaborate coded cipher to use in future communications. Digby would be 66, Browne 87 and Abingdon 406. Four days later Browne recorded that all the hay had been eaten up for four miles around. To keep the intrigue boiling Browne decided to dispense with Barnard, 'leaving his Master and me hand to hand'. Digby, impatient with Browne's delays, became suspicious. He wrote, 'I desire of you a positive resolution'. Alarmed by the tone of Digby's letter Browne used Barnard again, assuring Digby, through the preacher, he was 'resolved to go through with the proposition'. Digby, far from satisfied, wrote, 'In a word, if in return of this I may hear from you what and when you will do in plain terms'.

Browne realised the game was up and he could prevaricate no longer. 'Oh my Lord' he wrote, 'be more tender of the King's Honours and favours than thus to hang them out as Colours to invite treachery and disloyalty to come after them'.

Digby was furious and made a last desperate effort to use the intrigue to discredit Browne with his superiors. He allowed some of the correspondence to fall into Roundhead hands. Browne was prepared for this and Parliament were fully aware of every move their Major-General had made. Digby was reduced to calling Browne names and the Roundhead commander chided him, 'If I were a prostitute, my, Lord, as you call me, why did your Honour act the pimp'. Digby ordered a captured spy to be hanged and Browne ordered the death of five Royalist Irish prisoners in reprisal, informing Digby he would not be 'outdone by you, either in civility or justice'.

Within a few days of the last exchange, Major-General Crawford rode in from Reading. His troopers had bags of salt and other provisions over their saddle bows and one ton of match wound about their waists.

In late December, Captain Beckman, troopers of the Queen's Lifeguard accompanied by Lord Digby's German engineer, occupied Speaker Lenthall's house at Besselsleigh. The building was contained within a very strong quadrangular wall and Brown considered the house and its new occupants as 'very strong, and they will be ill-neighbours to us'. He sent a party of horse and foot under the command of Lieutenant Bosville to summon the garrison. To Bosville's surprise, the cavaliers meekly gave in. Beckman and the German engineer were escorted back to Abingdon as prisoners but the Lifeguard were allowed to return to Oxford. Much as Browne would have liked to garrison Besselsleigh he was forced to abandon it owing to the high desertion rate he suffered, the doors and walls were beaten down to prevent its future use to the Royalists.

Desertion was still high. Of Colonel Martin's only 30 troopers were left, Ayscough's men had deserted on the death of their officer and both Tyrrell's and Grenville's had returned home.

Heavy rain in late December and early January caused flooding in the river meadows around Abingdon, leaving only the old causeway high and dry. Prince Rupert openly boasted he would now retake Abingdon and with this in mind an attempt was made to break down Culham Bridge and fortify both the church and Lady Carey's house. On 11 January, early on a very foggy morning, Rupert, Maurice and Colonel Gage, with 800 horse and 1000 foot gained a foothold on the causeway. At the same time, Major Hatton Farmer, from Faringdon, attacked the Roundhead horselines at Drayton.

The town, alarmed by the twin attack, reacted quickly. After months of inactivity coupled with deprivation and starvation, the soldiers were eager to fight. Browne led the defence of the causeway and he ordered men into the flooded meadows on either side. 'Cheerfully' they 'marched through the water' to outflank the Cavaliers. Gaining the end of the causeway they came under fire from the two cannon the Royalists had placed to cover their work on the bridge. Browne sent back for two drakes to be hauled along the causeway and when they were brought into action they covered the men trying to stop the bridge demolition.

Tragically Colonel Gage was struck by a musket ball and died instantly. The death of the gallant colonel sent his men hurrying back from the bridge. 'Behind the said bridge was a great hill with many hedges' wrote a Roundhead survivor, 'which they lined with musketeers'. The engagement developed into a fire-fight which lasted four hours until at last seeing their plan had failed the Royalists returned to Oxford. Meanwhile the Faringdon contingent of Prince Rupert's horse had fared no better. Major Farmer was slain and his men fled back towards Faringdon. Harried all the way many died in street fighting within Faringdon itself.

Later, countrypeople brought carts to the scene about Culham. Three carts were loaded with dead and when these were filled the remaining bodies were unceremoniously flung into the Thames. The curious made their way to Abingdon after the battle. In the market square Brown hanged his Irish prisoners. As the church bells tolled for the funeral of a Roundhead officer killed that morning, each was turned off a ladder. 'The first of them' wrote an observer, 'as the ladder turned, cried God Zounds and died, all of them were lusty villains'. The day before an 'old man and my memory is short' carried a sheaf of notes for his final speech, to the scaffold. Archbishop Laud had his head struck from his body by order of Parliament. The attitude of both sides had hardened beyond any point of return, dark years still lay ahead.

CHAPTER FIFTEEN

OLD SOLDIERS - 'NEW MODEL' - APRIL 1645

'... if we beat the King ninety-nine times yet he is King still;
but if the King beat us once we should be hanged'.
The Earl of Manchester

In February 1643 a 'Committee of Both Kingdoms' was set up by
Parliament to plan the strategy of the war against the King. The
committee was made up of fourteen Members of Parliament, seven
Peers and four Commissioners represented the Kingdom of
Scotland. The committee soon had the responsibility of
maintaining three separate armies in the field.

At any one time the strength of these could be, the Earl of Essex
(a member of the committee), commanding 11 foot and 7 horse
regiments. Sir William Waller, commanding the South Eastern
Association with up to 14 foot, 8 horse and I dragoon regiment.
Lastly there was the Eastern Association, militarily, politically and
religiously powerful, commanded by the Earl of Manchester. It
was from the Eastern Association that Oliver Cromwell with his
famous 'ironsides' originated.

When the Allied armies went into winter quarters at the close of
1644, the country had been at war for two years. The state of
Berkshire was typical of the country as a whole. 'The whole
county being in a miserable condition, hardly a sheep, hen, hog,
oats, hay, wheat, or any other thing for man or beast to feed upon.'
Horses, so essential to the life of the countryside, were in
desperately short supply. Unable to purchase fresh mounts and
the supply of 'malignants' livestock running
out, the Roundheads were now leaving worn
out or wounded animals with local farmers and
taking their work horses.

By the close of that winter, William Ball, now a
colonel, was distressed enough to write to
Speaker Lenthall on the situation in the county,
'the soldiers having almost starved the people
where they quarter, and are half-starved

109

themselves for want of pay, and are become very desperate, raging about the country, breaking and robbing houses and passengers, and driving away sheep and other cattell before the owners faces'. Ball, a Berkshire committee member, warned Lenthall that the depredations of the soldiers were doing more danger to the county than the enemy. (1)

A number of churches were either robbed of their treasures or had their rooves stripped for lead to fashion musket balls. Vandalism in the name of Puritanism was rife. Private houses were prime targets for looters, Sir Humphrey Foster's house at Aldermaston was sacked by troopers accompanied by their officers.

Carriers through Berkshire became regular victims. One party paid the Royalist governor of Devizes a bond of £400 to travel with their goods. On reaching Newbury Boys rode out and levied the same fee for safe conduct. Once along the road troopers from Wallingford captured them and took men and goods to Wallingford. On arrival Blagge, the governor, exacted another £10 on each pack of cloth before allowing them to continue their journey.

Even Prince Rupert, the advocate of total war, was moved to note that the whole Nation was sliding 'into such animosity and cruelty, that all elements of charity, compassion and brotherly affection shall be extinguished'. Parliament passed an infamous act for any Irish prisoners taken to be hanged. Browne and Digby attempted to outshine each other in reprisals, later when Browne hanged five more Rupert ordered the death of thirteen Roundheads in return.

Parliament too could see the degeneration that internecine war produced. Their aim was still politically the same, to secure the King's person and put him from his advisers, they seemed no nearer their objective than the day war started. Three armies had failed to do this at Second Newbury, perhaps one modified army could succeed where they had failed.

After publicly attacking Manchester over the Newbury failure, Cromwell, prompted by others, put forward a fresh idea. All Members of Parliament holding a military rank should 'self-deny' their commissions A new army would be fashioned and its supreme commander would be appointed from outside Westminster. The Commons instructed the 'Committee of Both Kingdoms', 'to consider of a frame or model of the whole militia'. Zouch Tate moved the motion for implementing the Self-Denying Ordinance, the road was clear for the first British standing army; the New Model Army was born.

Sir Thomas Fairfax was appointed Commander-in-Chief and in April he journeyed from London to Windsor to set about organising his new command. Philip Skippon was appointed Major-General of foot. Skippon, a fanatical Puritan and experienced soldier, was held in high regard by the soldiers. This respect was to assist him in seeing the aims of the Cause through a difficult and dangerous period.

The New Model Army was to be trained at Windsor. It would consist of 22,000 men divided into 11 regiments of horse, each regiment 600 strong. One regiment of 1000 dragoons and 12 regiments of foot, each 1200 strong. The basis for the cavalry came from the Eastern Association and were thus Cromwell trained. Essex's cavalry was, by this time, very depleted and the whole force was reduced into three regiments. One regiment was given to Sir Robert Pye the younger; the Faringdon man had advanced a long way from the day he had raised a troop of horse for Parliament.

The onerous task of reducing the infantry regiments that existed and shaping the new ones fell to Skippon. The large number of officers serving would no longer be required and many would have to accept becoming ordinary men at arms. In early April 1645, Skippon arrived at Reading to execute Parliament's design on the regiments assembled there. (2)

On 5 April five regiments were drawn out into a field by Forbury. The orange-tawny colours of Essex's foot, Skippon's own regiment, Edward Aldrich's with their blue colours painted with a rampant lion, Henry Barclay's and Colonel Tyrrell's marched out. They were joined by the five red-coated companies of Lord Robart's regiment, their Chaplain Dr Calibut Downing,

Oliver Cromwell, founder of the New Model Army.

Rector of West Ilsley. If battle honours had decorated regimental colours in April 1645 these would carry such names as Edgehill, Reading siege, 1st Newbury, the Cornish Campaign, 2nd Newbury and many other battles and skirmishes. One officer was heard to comment that day 'he would rather lose his wife than his company'.

Townspeople looked on with misgivings as to the outcome of the muster. Wherever soldiers had gathered in Reading the talk had been of reduction, unemployment, lack of pay and their unsure future, even threats of mutiny and violence had been made.

Philip Skippon addressed each regiment individually so that none would miss his words. He told them of Parliament's plans for a new army and asked them to accept the situation. 'I know you will behave like men of honour and honesty' he said in summing up their future. They did, for after the muster common soldier, and now many an officer had elected to become such, 'orderly marcht thence in three reduc'd regiments, cheerful into three churches, where we forthwith inrolled every officer and souldier as they entered the new list, closed the books that evening, and with like diligence see the private souldier paid, and most of the reduc'd officers'. After penning this letter to his superiors, Skippon led his own regiment from Reading to Windsor. There he had mustered the soldiers of two more regiments, Sir Thomas Hogan's and Sir Miles Hobart's. They too were reduced into Skippon's own regiment, 'with the like quietness as at Reading'.

One week later Skippon was at Wokingham about the same business This time it was Colonel Weldon's Red Regiment raised in Kent. Reduced into the New Model this same regiment would later supply five companies to General George Monck. Monck's, in turn, became the Coldstream Guards. The Coldstream Guards are back at Windsor today.

The second regiment was that of James Holborne, once with the Earl of Essex. It was Holborne's along with Barclay's that held back the King at Caversham.

Probably the most dangerous and outrageous moves in military history were about to take place. The whole military arm of one side was to be reshaped in the middle of a war. It was while this re-shaping was taking place at Windsor and the Royalist army needed careful watching that Oliver Cromwell was sent into the field.

CHAPTER SIXTEEN

FARINGDON - WINTER 1644 - 5

'The guiltless Blood that shall be spilt God will require at your hands that have caused this Unnatural War'.
Lieutenant-Colonel Burges.

The King and Prince Rupert stayed overnight at Faringdon House on 22 November 1644. Donnington Castle, Wallingford Castle and Faringdon House were their last strongholds in Berkshire. The loss of Abingdon meant that Faringdon would now have the burden of more soldiers garrisoned from the Oxford Army. To protect their winter quarters it was seen that the defences of Faringdon would have to be improved and strengthened.

The King appointed Quarter-master General George Lisle as governor. Lisle had served in the foreign wars and against the Scots. He had been present at almost every major engagement of the Civil War and had succeeded to a regiment on the death of Richard Bolle at Alton. He commanded the Forlorn Hope at 1st Newbury and his gallantry at 2nd Newbury led to a Royalist tractarian saying, 'colonel George Lisle had no armour on besides courage and a good cause, and a good Holland shirt; for he seldom wears defensive arms'. Lisle's courage was never more evident than at his execution after the Second Civil War. Standing with his friend Sir Charles Lucas outside Colchester Castle, Lucas was killed first. Lisle kissed his dead face and then asked the soldiers to come closer. When told they would not miss he replied, 'comrades, I have been nearer than this and you missed me'.

Lisle and Rupert were old friends and the governor confessed to the Prince that the condition of Faringdon's defences worried him. He considered the place to be only one third fortified and the provisions inside dangerously low. The Prince agreed and Lisle, according to his 'wonted manner he did like a soldier'. Soon ditches were being cut, embankments being thrown up and sconces for the cannon set on

corners. Turf, cut into thick blocks, was stacked against buildings leaving only slits where there were formerly windows. Within a month Lisle felt confident enough to send raiding parties out into the countryside. Browne at Abingdon was soon writing to Parliament tof the prejudice we suffer by the new garrison at Faringdon, which stops all cattle and other provision usually coming by that way...' (l) Faringdon troops were not so successful in the Abingdon raid of January 1645 when they were chased back into their own lines.

While the New Model Army trained at Windsor and Parliament finally voted the Self-Denying Ordinance, Fairfax deliberately left vacant the position of Lieutenant-General of Horse. On 19 April 1645, Cromwell rode into Windsor to hand in his resignation as Parliament decreed. Within twentyfour hours orders arrived from Derby House, for Oliver Cromwell to remain in the field.

It has been claimed that Cromwell juggled the Self-Denying Ordinance to further his own ambitions. His aim was to retain command and to further the interests of the Independents who filled the ranks of the Ironsides. He may well have gambled that his services could not be lightly dispensed with or, and it is most likely, he simply left the matter in God's hands.

The 'New Noddle' as the Royalists contemptuously called the Parliamentary army was far from ready to take the field. The King however was, and it was his intention to move the Train of Artillery, currently in Oxford, to the safety of Hereford and Prince Rupert. Prince Maurice was to escort the train and for its movement he would need to lay hands on all available horses in the Oxford area.

Cromwell was ordered to command a strong contingent of horse and dragoons, to include men from Fairfax's, Whalley's and Holborne's, and to prevent or delay the artillery being moved. Browne at Abingdon wa instructed to lend all assistance he could from his base close to Oxford.

Moving swiftly from Watlington to Islip on 23 April Cromwell failed to surprise the Royalist Earl of Northampton's troops. Tradition has it that the Roundheads crossed the Cherwell near

116

Islip by ferry. The following day, now reinforced with troopers from Wilmot's and Palmer's horse, Northampton attacked. The fight took place near Islip Bridge and Northampton's three regiments were soundly beaten. The Queen's lost its colour, 40 Cavaliers were killed and a further 200 taken prisoner. The main prize was 400 horses. Royalist survivors fled towards Oxford, Woodstock and Bletchingdon House, it was towards the latter that Cromwell now pressed on.

The commander of Bletchingdon House was Colonel Francis Windebank who had served with Gage in the relief of Basing House. About 50 survivors from Islip made it to the house where they told exaggerated tales of the enemy strength, particularly in regard to Cromwells foot which was non-existent.

Thinking themselves safe at Bletchingdon, Windebank and his young wife had allowed women friends to visit the house. Influenced by their presence and by the refugee's stories, Windebank surrendered at the first summons.

The ease with which he had captured Bletchingdon surprised Cromwell. He saw Divine guidance in such a victory and he wrote, 'I did much doubt the storming of the house, it being strong and well manned., and I have few dragoons, and this not being my business; and yet we got it'. (2)

Windebank was allowed to march away with the honours of war but on arrival at Oxford he was arrested and court-martialed. He was charged with being 'faint-hearted' and on '3rd of May. Colonel Windebank was shotte to death' against the wall of Merton College. Later the King, who had ordered the trial, gave the widow a pension.

After Bletchingdon and Islip, Cromwell penned reports to London. The Self-Denying Ordinance was now in force but here was one MP with military rank demonstrating how successful he could be. While drawing off the horses to prevent them being used by Oxford he was also preventing farmers from working. He found time to criticise the practice of the army living off local people by free quarter, pointing out that this only antagonised them.

Oxford now began to react to the Roundhead presence. On Saturday troops were sent from Wallingford to bring Northampton's regiment up to better strength and infantry arrived in Oxford from Faringdon.

Staying north of the Royalist capital, Cromwell pushed westward. At Bampton-in-the-Bush they met their first real opposition. Colonel John Fiennes had already been detached to go in pursuit of Royalist horse that had been seen nearby. Fiennes caught up with them near (3) Faringdon capturing colours and taking a number of prisoners.

Now Cromwell, his force divided, was faced with superior numbers of foot and horse. The Cavalier horses scattered by the foot, on their way from Oxford to Radcot, managed to get back into Bampton. They 'barricaded up the town' and refused a summons, forcing Cromwell to send in a night attack which was driven out with heavy losses. Reinforced by the returning Fiennes, Cromwell launched a second attack the next morning and after losing over 100 men the Royalists surrendered. The remainder were sent back to Abingdon as prisoners. Cromwell now asked Browne to supply him with reinforcements of infantry with the intention of reducing Faringdon.

During the evening of 28 April the Roundheads crossed Radcot Bridge and encamped close to Faringdon. The Council of War at Oxford were aware of Cromwell's position but still not clear as to his intention. 'Cromwell is now laying at Stanford and other places next to Faringdon with six regiments of horse and four troops of dragoons, expecting the coming of Colonel Roydon's thither'.

'Roydon' was Sir Marmaduke Rawdon. A Lieutenant-Colonel in 1642 in the Red Regiment of the London Trained Bands, he had joined the King's side at the outbreak of war. Raising a regiment of musketeers at his own expense he had successfully helped in the defence of Basing House. Basing had foolishly elected to become a Roman Catholic stronghold, excluding all Protestants.

Rawdon, his musketeers and a number of horse and foot were thus expelled for their faith. If indeed Cromwell was aware of this and awaiting them he could not have known they had not yet left Basing.

The loss of so many horses altered the Royalists plans. Sending artillery to Hereford was now impossible and therefore the Prince was instructed to come to Oxford. Goring was ordered up from the west where he was currently laying siege to Taunton. Both were asked to sweep up as many draught horses as they could lay their hands on during their journeys.

Meanwhile, Fairfax had been told to march the New Model to the relief of Taunton. He arrived at Reading on 30 April, that morning Cromwell launched his first attack on Faringdon House.

Within hours of arriving by Faringdon the Roundheads had secured the town, the garrison had retired into their earthworks which encompassed the house and Parish Church. The usual courteous moves had been made but either confidence or haste caused Cromwell to be less polite than was the practice. His summons threatened 'the utmost extremity of war' should the garrison refuse.

Lisle was absent and his position was taken by Lieutenant-Colonel Roger Burges of Sir John Owen's Regiment of Foot. Burges rejected the summons and Cromwell was stung to warn him, 'if God gives you into my hands, I will not spare a man of you, if you put me to the storm'. Loftily Burges replied, '... we would have you know you are not now at Bletchingdon'.

During these verbal preliminaries, the reinforcements from Abingdon arrived, Pickering's Regiment of Foot. Well suited to fight beside Cromwell, their colonel was a fanatical Independent. Browne had however only been able to spare between five and six hundred men for fear of his garrison being attacked.

Cromwell decided on a night attack timed for

three o'clock on the morning of 30 April. The attack was launched on three separate points of the defences at the same time. Scaling ladders were thrown up the walls and men dashed up them led by their officers. Burges, on the wall, personally threw one ladder back with the aid of a pike. Henry Cannon, captain to one of Whalley's troops, had been one of the first up a ladder and the first down. He lay floundering in the mud and darkness and was still there when captured. Many Roundheads died in that first storming and those driven back retired so fast that the ladders were left against the walls. Captain Jennings of Pickering's was killed and Cornet George Scale and Quartermaster Richard Smith of Holborne's wounded. Later their petition for pay for their adventure at Faringdon was personally underwritten by Skippon for the sum of £5. 16s. 8d. (4)

Burges managed to get a message out and delivered to the King at Oxford. He assured the King that he could hold out for five days at least. More welcome was the news that at least 100 men of Vaughan's party, thought to have been killed or captured at Bampton, had managed to get back into Faringdon with their weapons.

At daybreak both sides called a truce and there was a 'gathering together of dead bodies'. Cromwell, impressed by the stoutness of the defence, he had lost 14 men, became more civil in his tone and offered an equal exchange of prisoners.

As the Parliamentarian forces began to settle in around Faringdon for a protracted siege, Abingdon was notified by scouts that Royalist forces were approaching the area quite fast. Browne informed Cromwell who was about to depart for Newbury and a meeting with Fairfax. Parliament sources were not certain as to Goring's whereabouts but, expecting he may head for Berkshire, Cromwell and Browne were instructed to co-operate to prevent incursion there.

Goring was in fact quite close. He had mustered his army at Marlborough by 2 May and late the same afternoon he was joined at Lambourn by Rawdon. Rawdon and his followers had been attacked as they crossed the Kennet between Thatcham and Newbury. The Roundhead Colonel, John Butler, had dogged them and at one stage they had tried to seek shelter in Donnington Castle. Boys had refused them entry for fear of drawing down a further siege. Butler had managed to capture a few stragglers but he had withdrawn when Goring and Rawdon met at Lambourn.

Fairfax arrived at Newbury with the army as Goring was mustering at Marlborough, Cromwell with a small escort joined him there. Butler's prisoners revealed that Goring's intention was to beat up Cromwell's quarters at Faringdon. Cromwell hurried back to Faringdon and immediately set about securing his lines. A small fort had been set up at Radcot Bridge to secure the Thames crossing and Cromwell sent Major Bethel with a troop of horse to ensure its safety. Unbeknown to Bethel, a detachment of Goring's, under Lieutenant-Colonel Scroop, had taken the post and now lined the hedges on the Oxford side hoping to ambush Roundhead patrols.

It was dark when Bethel arrived at the Bridge and he led his men over and a short way along the Clanfield Road. When the Cavaliers opened fire Bethel was the first thrown from his horse and a number of his troopers were killed In the fight two colours were captured and a number of prisoners taken. The Cavaliers pressed on to take the earthwork fort, the bridge and Radcot House. With the Royalists so close Cromwell was forced to abandon further attempts on Faringdon House and he withdrew towards Newbury and the safety of the New Model Army.

All casualty reports, particularly Civil War ones, are exaggerated. Cromwell certainly succeeded in his mission of preventing the King's artillery moving from Oxford. At Faringdon he is said to have captured 180 Cavaliers besides a number of officers. On the other hand did 'Master Cromwell's 1000 horse' really get shamefully beaten by 400 of His Majesties' at Radcot Bridge? Certainly Fairfax drew his army further south than he had originally planned and Faringdon could justly claim they had defied Cromwell - and won.

CHAPTER SEVENTEEN

THE CLUBMEN - AUGUST 1645

'if you offer to plunder or take our cattle.
You may be sure we'll give you battle'.
A Clubmen slogan

Wearing white ribbons as badges, carrying white banners bearing
the above motto, Berkshire's Clubmen gathered on Compton
Down, near Ilsley, in August 1645.

The title, 'Clubmen' derived from the crude weapons carried by
the militant followers of the movement. Strongest in the West
Country, the uprising reached its peak in late 1645. Inspired by
the grievances of the farmers and yeomen and often encouraged
by the Royalists, particularly the priests, it was meant to be a
popular neutral protest. Whole counties banded together to resist
the demands of both sides.

The non-stop demands for contributions to support garrisons, the
disruption of harvests, damage to crops and livestock, dislocation
of markets and the frequent impressment of much needed farm
labour, contributed to the Movement's growth. Only the month
previous to the Compton meeting Berkshire was asked to impress
500 more soldiers, at the same time Parliament had voted
Ordinance for the relief of the county.

'18th July 1645. The Lords and Commons assembled in
Parliament, duly 'considering the miserable condition of the
Counties of Oxon, Bucks, Berks, and Southampton, and other the
neighbouring Counties, by reason of continual Plunderings and
Alarums from the Garrisons of Oxon, Basing, Winchester,
Wallingford, Banbury, Newark, and other places adjacent in the
Enemies power, ...' (1)

At first the Clubmen were content to aid deserters and mete out
summary justice on looters but soon their demands fringed on
political and religious matters.

Both factions made attempts to win Clubmen support, such

efforts met with little success. George Goring, commander of perhaps the worst disciplined troops from either side, armed clubmen and activly sought their support. Rupert failed to enlist the aid of the Somerset followers. Massey, Parliamentry govenor of Gloucester, managed to recruit some to his side.

Armed clashes began to occur between troops and Clubmen. The Wilts', Hants' and Sussex Clubmen were dispersed with violence at Winchester by Colonel Norton. Prayers and sermons had been said at Basing in their favour and for a while the garrison hoped the movement would work in their favour. By July Fairfax was made aware of 'the great danger from the Club-risers; who would suffer neither contributions or victuals to be carried to the Parliament's garrisons'. The Dorset leaders requested safe-conduct to carry their petition to the King and both Houses of Parliament, Fairfax refused them. Later, at Hambledon Hill, Cromwell and his brother-in-law Disbrowe, ruthlessly broke up a large meeting, killing 60 and taking 400 prisoners.

Cromwell described them as 'poor silly creatures'. His letters show he was very much against the despoilation of the countryside by the constant demands of the soldiery but in the Clubmen movement he and other Army Grandees saw a far deeper significance. Political awareness was already developing within the army; a third political force would make future settlement of the Kingdom even more difficult for them to control.

The Berkshire Clubmen appear to have been far less militant than their counterparts in other counties. Their first large scale meeting, held on Compton Down on 12 August 1645, was attended by two members of the Berkshire Committee. Mr John Hamilton of Tilehurst, Chief Constable for the Reading Hundred, was observed handing out tickets for the next meeting. He was later arrested and when the Clubmen leaders petitioned for his release accompanied by their Declaration and designed to be read by King and Parliament, clearly shows their demands, hopes and fears. It also demonstrates the class of people involved in its Organisation. Little or nothing is heard of the movement in the county

Seventeenth century Caliver man.
From Jacob De Gheyn's 'The Exercise of Arms'.

after the August meetings. Probably, like the rest of the country it became, through force of circumstances more Parliamentary in its loyalties.

'The Peaceable MEETING ON COMPTON DOWN, near Ilsley, to the COMMITTEE FOR BERKSHIRE. 1645, August 12.

Whereas we the knights, gentlemen, freeholders, and others the inhabitants of the County of Berks, who have been for a long time overpressed with the insupportable burdens and contrary commands of the many garrisons and several armies both of the King and of the Parliament .. lately had a meeting to advise which way we might in the fairest way have but a livlihood and yield a competent proportion to the said garrisons until we might hear of a happy issue of our addresses both to the King and Parliament by our humble petitions now prepared and forthwith to be presented, to which purpose we then gave directions to the High Constables of several Hundred.... to give notice to the several inhabitants in the said Hundreds to give us a second meeting to the affect promised, and understanding that for the execution of this request your Honours have - peradventure upon some misapprehensions - imprisoned John Hamilton of Tilehurst, the High Constable of the Hundred of Reading, we with one general consent earnestly desire that he may be speedily released.'

Enclosed with the above was their actual declaration.

'DECLARATION.

We. the miserable inhabitants of the County of Berks... foreseeing famine and utter desolation will inevitably fall upon us our wives and children, unless God of His Infinite mercy shall... be graciously pleased to put a period to those sad distractions are unanimously resolved to join in petitioning his Majesty and the two Houses of Parliament for a happy peace and accommodation of the present differences without further effusion of Christian blood.... In the meantime we with one heart and mind declare that we really intend to the utmost hazard of our lives and fortunes:

1. To defend and maintain the true Reformed Protestant religion.
2. To join with and assist one another in the

mutual defence of our laws liberties and properties against all plunderers and all other unlawful violence whatsoever.

3. We do hereby resolve and faithfully promise each to each other that if any person or persons whatsoever, who shall concur with and assist us in those our resolutions happen to suffer in his person or estate in execution of the premises it shall be as the suffering of the generality and reparation shall be made to the party suffering according to his damage, and in the case of loss of life provision shall be made for his wife and children and all this to be done at a conscionable rate and allowance to the uttermost ability of all the associates,

4. Lastly we do declare all such unworthy of our assistance as shall refuse to join with us in the prosecution of these our just intentions.

The organisers also included an invitation to the members of the Berkshire Committee to attend the next meeting with the petition.

'1645 August 12. Whereas we are informed that the High Constable of Reading Hundred is lately imprisoned for sending forth tickets according to the general direction at the meeting on lisley Downs, when you were both present, it is earnestly desired by the like general consent that you would be pleased to repair together with Mr llsley and Mr Wilder to present the petition directed to the Honourable the Committee at Reading for his releasement. You are both earnestly desired to be at the next meeting which is appointed on Tuesday next, the 19th August instant. ' (2)

CHAPTER EIGHTEEN

DONNINGTON CASTLE - 1644-46

No sooner than the Parliament forces left Newbury in November 1644, than the irrepressible Boys and his garrison were in action again. They rode into Newbury, pulled the Mayor and other prominent citizens from their beds, and attempted to return with them to Donnington. They proposed to hold the prisoners for ransom but the arrival of a large troop of Roundhead horse forced them to abandon them.

The castle was now in a very dilapidated state, its towers gone and walls beaten down. While not wishing to call down another siege Boys was quite happy to continue raiding the country around and hindering western trade with London. They ranged as far as Basing, where, on one occasion, they beat up the enemy quarters carrying off a Colour, two officers and seven soldiers.

In the autumn of 1645 Cromwell detached Colonel Dalbier with his regiment of 300 horse to lay siege to the castle. Dalbier, a Dutch engineer, had served in several engagements including First Newbury. Left out of the Model Army and later, generally neglected, he joined the Earl of Holland's Royalist rising. In November 1645 all this was far in the future. The Berks', Bucks' and Oxon Committee were directed to unite their forces to assist Dalbier and for the first time money was voted for the reduction of Donnington Castle.

On 6 November Dalbier led the Associated Counties armed forces to Newbury where he was joined by Colonel Thomas Bettesworth, High Sheriff of Hants', with his Hampshire levies. Sussex provided 200 foot and Surrey furnished five companies of foot and a troop of horse. The Berkshire horse were led by the freshly promoted Major John Blagrave and was 300 strong. Infantry soldiers had been drawn out of Windsor and marched to Newbury commanded by Captain Robert Voisey. Even with such numbers Dalbier still hesitated to undertake that which Cromwell

General Fairfax.

had described as 'such a knotty piece of business.' Dalbier gathered his reinforcements at a rendezvous near Aldermaston and set down about Donnington early in December.

Parliament were far from satisfied with Dalbier's dilatory attitude and yet another committee was set up to look into the matter. Dalbier's excuse to the committee was the particularly hard winter which had set in. The weather conditions had forced him to quarter his men rather than encamp them about the defences. Some of those quartered billeted in Newbury Church and caused a great deal of damage to the fabric of the building, particularly the roof where lead was stripped for musket balls; the church had also been used as a prison for Royalists captured.

The lull of early 1645 had enabled Boys to well stock the castle with provisions and to render maintenance to the defences. Parts of Donnington Village had been burnt down and other villages and barns had been burnt in the area to prevent the Roundheads gaining shelter. Lessons learned from previous sieges led to better defence against mortars and when Dalbier finally arrived he discovered he could merely hinder rather than take the garrison.

The Spring of 1646 allowed Dalbier and his Roundheads to take the field again. One of the first incidents occurred when a party of horse surprised Cavaliers drinking at Boxford. Four or five houses were burnt down by Boys in a pointless reprisal. Dalbier had been chosen for the task of reducing Donnington as he was an acknowledged expert in the science of taking a well defended position, he had been present for some time at Basing House.

Tunnels were started and trenches zigzagged towards the earthworks as was the 'modern' fashion. Seven companies of foot were engaged in constructing a redoubt on the 'side of May Pole Hill'. Boys became so concerned about the approaching trenches that he ordered a counter attack out of his concealed sally-port. Observing the enemy had withdrawn its cavalry screen of the pioneers he launched the attack at 7 o'clock in the morning. At first the Roundheads broke and ran but soon a stiff resistance began. Boys

129

tried to keep the fighting confined to the trenches where the horse could not operate. Sending in reinforcements the Roundheads were forced to vacate the ditches to the Cavaliers who, according to one eye-witness fought 'like divils'. Over eighty Roundheads were killed in the skirmish.

Dalbier, despite Derby House and its censures, was made of sterner material than previous besiegers of Donnington. He regained his positions and was able to site his mortar piece within range of the Gatehouse. This fearsome weapon may well have been the 'One Great Mortar Piece' used previously with dreadful affect at Basing. Stones, logs bound with iron, red hot balls and granadoes could be fired from these siege weapons. Seventeen large missiles were recorded to have been fired at Donnington. The stonework of the castle was further damaged but the earthworks of the star-fort were still the principle obstacle against storming.

Dalbier's persistence however was beginning to pay off. The defenders powder supply was running low and in March 1646 Dalbier acquainted Colonel Boys with the deteriorating position of the Royalist cause in other parts of the country. Appreciating that relief was highly unlikely to appear again, Boys approached Dalbier with a view to obtaining safe-conduct for two officers to leave the castle and inform the King of the position and seek instructions. Dalbier agreed and Captains' Osborn and Donne made the journey to Oxford. The King saw the hopelessness of his loyal garrisons position and told the officers that Boys should see the best terms he could, and surrender.

Colonel John Boys, resourceful and audacious to the last, made excellent terms. The actual terms were printed and published and they are well worth quoting in full as they mirror the attitude of victor and vanquished in the English Civil War and demonstrate Boys's canny negotiating ability.

'1. It is agreed upon, that Sir John Boys, knight, Governour of Dennington Castle aforesaid, shall march according to the Articles insuing agreed upon (that is to say) upon Wednesday morning next, being the first day of April, by 6 of the clock, the

Governour, with all his officers, Gentlemen, and Souldiers, are then to march out with Cullers flying and Drums beating, the Governour with 4 horses and arms, and every Field Officer with 2, and every Capt. 1, the Lieut-Col. of horse with two horses and arms, and the other officers and reformado officers of horse with 1 horse and arms apiece, 100 of the foot soldiers to march with their arms two miles, and the rest to march without, towards Wallingford, and then 50 to lay down their arms, and the other 50 to march with Cullers flying, drums beating, light matches, bullets in their mouth, and bandeliers fill'd with powder.

2. That if any officer or souldier in this garrison hath been in the Parliament service, shall receive the equal benefit comprised in these articles.

3. That what officer or souldier late of this garrison shall desire to go beyond the sea, shall have a Passe to go to London, or to what place they desire, within the Parliament's quarters to procure the same accordingly.

4. That all Officers and Souldiers, late of this garrison who desire to go to their own mansions or place of residence and several dwellings, have a free passe to do so, without being molested or pressed to any oath, provided that they be engaged never to take up arms against the Parliament.

5. That there shall be a safe conduct granted to Wallingford.

6. That there shall be two carts with teams, provided by the time appointed, the one to carry Sir John Boys' baggage, the other to carry the Officers.

7. That the Governour, Officers, and Souldiers, late of Dennington Castle aforesaid, shall at the time deliver up the Castle aforesaid to Col. Dulbier for the use of the Parliament, with all the Ordnance, Arms, Ammunition, and Provision therein (except that what is before expressed), without embezzling the arms or ammunition, or demolishing the works.
8. That the prisoners now in Dennington

Castle shall upon signing of these articles be delivered forth and set at liberty.

9. That the wounded Souldiers of the Castle shall have liberty to be left in Newbury or elsewhere the Governour pleases, and to have present passes, that after their recovery they may go to their severall mansions or dwellings without interuption or molestation.

Signed

Colonel Martin
Major Rynes For Colonel Dulbier
Major Collingwood.
Major Bennet
Capt. Osborn For Sir John Boys
Capt. Gregory (1)

CHAPTER NINETEEN

NORTH BERKSHIRE - NOVEMBER 1645 - JUNE 1646

> To Farrington garrison I came, a stranger
> amongst those eminent soldiers: ....
> > John Gwyn.

The summer of 1645 had been one long catalogue of defeat for the Royalists. After the battle of Naseby, (14 June) Fairfax had marched his victorious army south, his intention, the relief of Taunton.

On Thursday, 26 June, they quartered at Lechlade. One of the Roundhead troops of horse had brushed with Faringdon Cavaliers who were caught gathering contributions in Lechlade. The following day, after an exchange of fire, Highworth surrendered. Malmesbury, a Roundhead garrison, was asked to supply a small force to occupy Highworth and once this was done, Fairfax continued on with a forced march into the West Country.

Taunton was relieved and Goring's army defeated at Langport, (10 July). Goring had armed the local Clubmen but this had had little effect on his fortunes. Prince Rupert surrendered Bristol, (10 September) and Basing House at last fell to Cromwell in a storming which resulted in a terrible loss of life (14 October). Even now Donnington, Wallingford and Faringdon still held out for the King.

By late November the West Country was firmly under Parliamentary control. The Roundhead Colonel Nicholas Devereux felt however that while Faringdon and Radcot remained, a threat was posed to the security of Wiltshire. Already there had been one incursion. Horse, 1200 strong, led by Sir John Causfield, had been raised from Oxford, Banbury, Wallingford, Boarstall and Faringdon. They had mounted one large raid into Wilts' 'to gather subsistance'.

Devereux, while not prepared to initiate a storming of either Radcot or Faringdon, planned to contain them by stationing troops in Lechlade. Captain William Moore was commissioned to occupy and fortify the town. Colonel Morgan, his Gloucester horse billeted in the district, was directed to support Moore should occasion arise.

On 20 November, Colonel Palmer, commander of Radcot, was made aware of Roundhead activity in Lechlade. He sent Captain Aytwood and 30 horse with instructions to either prevent, or at least delay, any construction of defences the Parliamentarians had in mind. On approaching Lechlade they were seen and fired upon, Aytwood receiving a bullet in the thigh. Bearing their wounded officer away, cursing the enemy, his men promised to return.

That evening they carried out their promise. Led by Lieutenant Colonel Nott (wounded previously when Fairfax was at Lechlade), and Major Duett, 120 horse and 100 foot, headed towards Lechlade. The force included troopers of the King's Lifeguard.

Moore, alerted by his sentries of Nott's approach, immediately sent for the Gloucester horse. He ordered his musketeers to line the hedges and walls bordering the narrow approach road into Lechlade. The Cavaliers were almost into the town before they were subjected to the withering cross fire of the concealed musketeers. A number were killed before Nott could group them into defensive positions and a fierce fire-fight developed.

The arrival of Morgan's troopers compelled Nott to withdraw and the fighting continued over the fields all the way back to Radcot. Once under the banked defences and protection of Radcot's guns, Nott turned and counter attacked. Duett was slain and Nott captured along with a number of his fellow Cavaliers. Satisfied with the action the Roundheads withdrew to Lechlade with their prisoners. Nott, considered to be a thorn in Parliament's side and described as 'a most malevolent man', was sent under a strong escort to London five days later.

Although the Royalists had been beaten, the action highlighted Devereux's argument that Radcot and Faringdon were still a danger. Browne at Abingdon was no less aware of the threat the garrison posed and even more concern was felt by Dalbier blockading Donnington Castle. Writing in January 1646, Dalbier stated quite firmly that the 300 horse at Faringdon, the 200 horse at Wallingford and the 50 at Donnington could, if they wanted, rendezvous without his knowledge. He added, should they be so minded as to mount 200 musketeers behind such a powerful body of horse, Newbury could easily be lost to Parliament. Dalbier also feared, although considering it unlikely, that the Royalists could fortify Compton Beauchamp, thus adding to his problems. The Royalists held no such bold intentions - for them the war was almost lost.

In March 1646 the Oxford Royalists made their last attempt on Abingdon. Colonel Payne had taken over as governor in place of Major-General Browne and it is from Payne's letter to Browne, written on March 2, that we learn the details.

'Last night the enemy drew out of Oxford a party of 1000 horse, and all the strength they could make of foot', his letter begins, 'they came between Thrupp and Norcot to Barton House, and kept covert until daylight'. Barton House is now a fire blackened shell, and it was from here the Royalists heard the drums beating revielle. They knew the 'out sentinels' would be called in at this time and the way would be clear for a surprise attack. They attacked the Spurr and other points and over 300 managed to enter Abingdon and occupy 'Abby-guard, Spurr-guard, Wayne-guard, and Barre'. They pressed forward almost reaching the town prison.

The aim of the infantry was to secure Bore Bridge and admit the horse. There was a redoubt at Bore Lane end and it was to this emplacement that Payne led his own soldiers. Another party was sent to defend Wayne-guard and on both fronts the Royalist pikemen were forcing back the Roundhead horse. Major Blundell and Colonel Washburn counter attacked and managed to prise the Cavaliers from their newly won positions. The Roundheads lost two captains, Taylor and Madocks, killed in the fighting but

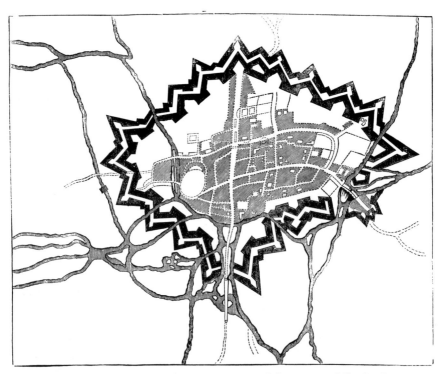

Plan of the Civil War defences of the city of Oxford.

several Royalists were taken prisoner. A Roundhead quartermaster was dangerously wounded and Blundell receive a halberd thrust in his leg.

The Sussex men holding Ock Bridge ran away and it was only the timely arrival of fresh Parliament horse that saved the bridge from capture. Colonel Washburn's counter attack was having its effect and although his great bay horse was killed under him he managed to push the Royalist infantry out of the town. Large numbers of dead and dying horses blocked the free movement of troops within the town and made the counter attacks slower than the Roundheads would have liked. After fierce house to house and street to street fighting the unsupported Cavalier foot had no option other than to withdraw. (2)

After the unsuccessful attempt at dislodging the enemy at Abingdon, the King realised it could not be long before Oxford would be threatened again. He decided, as a precaution, to disperse a large proportion of his horse into the remaining garrisons. On 3 April a decoy party was sent towards Nuneham while 600 horse made their way towards Faringdon by way of Cumnor and Fyfield. Included in the column was Sir William Compton's Regiment of Horse which had relieved Banbury during the Second Newbury campaign.

Payne ordered Colonel Betsworth to Nuneham but on discovery of the main Royalist horse on the other side of Abingdon had the Colonel return. At the same time Payne sent dragoons to harry the column in the hope of delaying it long enough for Betsworth to return. The Royalists had already quartered in and around Faringdon when Payne led his attack. A number of Cavaliers were slain in the first action and there was fierce fighting in the streets of Faringdon. 200 Horse managed to escape the confusion of the street fighting and escaped, they regrouped in a meadow which lay between the two coxwell villages.

On the arrival of the superior numbers of Roundhead horse, they attempted a parley. A skirmish developed and this turned into a full scale fight in which the Royalists were totally defeated. A large number surrendered and were taken as prisoners back to Abingdon. On the arrival of so many, Payne was at a loss to know what to do with them. Some he reported were willing to change sides, others promised never to take up arms again while many simply wanted to return to their homes. Of the remainder he cold-bloodedly had no doubts as to their future, 'there are some Irishmen taken, which, I doe intend to hang up tomorrow morning'. (3)

Within days of the skirmish at Coxwell, Troops under Colonel Sanderson were ordered from Lechlade and Standlake, to block up Radcot. Malmesbury sent 300 foot to Highworth, there they joined with others, collected a number of cannon and marched on Faringdon.

On 27 April the King secretly left Oxford and travelled to Newark, there he gave himself into the hands of the Scottish army. Not knowing quite what to do with him they made him an

honoured prisoner.

The day following the King's departure from Oxford, Marmaduke Rawdon died at Faringdon, the old Cavalier was 64 years of age and still in the service of his King. They buried him under a black stone slab in the nave of Faringdon Church.

By 3 May Fairfax had completely surrounded Oxford with his New Model Army. Colonel Barkstead was placed in control of the Berkshire side of the City and Colonel Payne was sent to block up Wallingford.

To ensure a free passage of his supplies over the Thames, Fairfax sent Colonel Cook to assist the troops at Radcot, they were to secure the Bridge and take the house. Earthworks, known locally as 'The Garrison', can still be seen on the Oxford side of the bridge and to the west of the road. Summoned to surrender on 11 May, the house finally capitulated on 24 May when grenades begin to fall through the roof. (4) Wallingford Castle was summoned at the same time as Radcot

Sir Robert Pye was detached to command the troops charged with taking Faringdon House, Pye's home. Faringdon was summoned on the same day as the other garrisons, the summons was rejected.

John Gwyn, a Royalist who served throughout the war, was at Faringdon and in his Memoirs described scenes from the final days. (5) Gwyn narrowly escaped death on several occasions according to his 'memoirs'. He was bending down on the stairs of Faringdon House when a cannon ball penetrated the building, striking the wall close to him. A fragment of stone struck his leg and he claimed that the leg broke in that place on three later occasions.

Courtney told Gwyn of a number of Cavalier deserters that having defected were locked into the town pest house which lay some way south of the present town. On seeing that the loop-holes for the muskets in the barricaded pest house left little room for the occupants to view an approach Gwyn led a daring attack to get the Cavaliers back. Crouching under the line of fire and getting close to the rampart of slabs of turf piled about the building,

138

Gwyn's men poured fire into the building. The guards asked for quarter and the deserters were herded back towards Faringdon House. As the party approached the house the Roundheads counter-attacked. The Cavalier support of horse was slow in coming and it took a dozen of Gwyn's friends to save him from death or certain capture.

During another sally out, while jumping over the entrenchments, a Mr Juell and a corporal were killed. They were struck by a cannon ball on the very spot where Gwyn landed a few seconds after them.

One sally developed into a full-scale fight which, according to Courtney's watch, lasted four hours. Gwyn claimed that 300 of the garrison took on 1500 of the enemy, drove them from their earthworks into the town then forced them from a fortified house with artillery fire. Once in the open fields the enemy were routed again.

From Newcastle, the King sent a letter on 10 June concerning the Oxford garrisons. 'Having resolved to comply with the designes of the Parliaments in everything which may be good for the subjects' he wrote, '... to require you upon honourable conditions, to quit those Townes and Castles, and Forts, intrusted by you to us, and to disband all the forces under your severall Commands.' (6)

Lisle and Burges, being in Oxford at the time of the negotiations, were able to affect Faringdon's surrender as part of the Oxford Articles, Lisle insisting on the same benefits. The surrender Aricles were read to Parliament on 23 June 1646, Article 24 dealt with Faringdon;

'That the Garrisons of Farringdon shall be rendered to his Excellency Sir Thomas Fairfax, and the Governor, Gentlemen, Souldiers, and all other of what quality soever within those Garrisons, shall enjoy the benefit of these Articles in every particular which may concern them, they rendering the Garrisons accordingly as Oxford'.

An eyewitness to the surrender of Oxford wrote of the soldiers marching out at twelve o'clock on Wednesday 24 June, it 'being a very rainy day'. It was probably raining at Faringdon. (7)

Wallingford, that persistent thorn in Parliaments side, was the last Oxford garrison to surrender. The Cavaliers from Wallingford had ranged far and wide over Berkshire, creating havoc on the Roundhead supply lines. Colonel Dalbier had been ordered to block up the Berkshire side of the town and he had billeted his troops in Wallingford. Fairfax was compelled to send a whole division to summon the castle. His own regiment was reinforced with that of Colonel Lilburne's. Blagge, the governor, knowing Oxford had surrendered and seeing the large force about the walls agreed to negotiate. It was not until 22 July that he agreed a surrender for Wednesday 29 July. (8)

There were fifteen Articles to the surrender and after being sealed and signed by the officers representing both sides, Blagge faced a mutiny from officers wishing to continue the struggle. The governor allowed the Roundheads into the garrison a day earlier than previously planned and Roundhead troops under Lieutenant Colonel Jackson forcibly kept the factions apart and supervised an orderly take over of the town. (9)

CHAPTER TWENTY

COLONEL SIR ROBERT PYE - A BERKSHIRE ROUNDHEAD

"...He was esteemed a fine gentleman
By all who knew him......
Pye's gravestone, Faringdon Parish Church

In 1623 Sir Robert Pye (the elder) purchased the Manor of Faringdon from Sir John Wentworth. The purchase included the large rambling Elizabethan, Faringdon House. Also known as 'the Place', the building stood just behind the Parish Church of All Saints.

Pye had benefited from the patronage of the Royal favourite, the Duke of Buckingham. Pye became Remembrancer of the Exchequer in 1621 and was Member of Parliament for Woodstock. At about the time of his appointment to Government office, his son, Robert, was born. (1)

The young Robert Pye grew up to be a strong-minded, independent son, totally opposed to his father's Court Party sympathies. He was probably influenced politically by his wife's family, the Hampdens. In 1641 Robert Pye married Anne Hampden, daughter of John Hampden, known to history as 'The Patriot'. This also made him a distant kinsman of the later powerful Cromwell family, his mother-in-law was Cromwell's aunt. Where Pye and Cromwell would fall out in the years to come was over religion, Pye was a Presbyterian and Cromwell an Independent.

During the summer of 1642, when the country was faced with imminent Civil War, Robert Pye was one of the many young gentlemen who 'signed on' at the Guildhall in London. By leaving their names and addresses, the troops of Roundhead horse were raised and Pye became a captain in Essex's army.

141

Pye lost no time in serving Parliament. In September he arrested a man who 'had taken up arms against Parliament' sending the prisoner to Tanfield Vachell, Sheriff of Berkshire, and another kinsmen. He requested the prisoner be sent to London.

In October he was reported to be in Oxford with his troop of horse and he fought at Edgehill with other independant troop captains answerable to Essex. (3) By October 22, there was a marginal entry in Prince Rupert's diary, 'Pye was an enemy'. (4)

In January 1643 the elder Pye fell foul of Parliament. A letter, written to Sir Edward Nicholas, the King's Secretary of State was intercepted and read to the House of Commons. In it Pye stated that his sons actions in taking up arms against the King were against his wishes and done without his knowledge or consent. He claimed he would no longer support his son financially or otherwise. What was worse, the letter revealed Pye was secretly contributing funds to the Royalist cause. It was only Hampden's influence that saved the elder Pye from expulsion from the House, or worse, and he thereafter remained quietly in London carrying out his Parliamentary duties. (5)

On 24 Febuary 1643, Pye's troop were operating near Brill, They ran into a party of Cavaliers, killing two and capturing sixteen. The prisoners, including a colonel and captain by the name of Chamberlaine, were confined in Windsor Castle. (6) In August Captain Chamberlaine was released only to be killed a few days later.

Undoubtedly Pye served with Essex at the siege of Reading ard he was to stay with the Earl's army until the formation of the New Model. On the return from the relief of Gloucester Pye led the musketeers that surprised Cirencester where he was wounded. During the summer of 1644, now a colonel, he served in the Cornish Campaign. He captured Taunton Castle which surrendered at the first summons. At Tiverton his regiment mustered three troops and contained 32 officers and 203 troopers. (7) With the rest of the cavalry, Pye escaped capture in Cornwall when the infantry were left to surrender.

With the formation of the New Model Army, Robert Pye was one of the few officers of high rank from Essex's army that received a regiment, his three troops being brought up to six. Some of his company officers in the new regiment were to become well known figures in future events. His major was Matthew Tomlinson and his captain's Margery, Knight, Barry and Rawlins. Tomlinson had served in Essex's Lifeguard and had been stationed at Abingdon in March 1645. At least two of the captains were known personally to Oliver Cromwell. Of Margery, Cromwell had written, 'I had rather have a plain russet-coated captain that knows what he fights for, and loves what he knows, than that which you call gentleman and is nothing else'. On requesting that Rawlins be commissioned captain, Cromwell had written to Fairfax, declaring he considered Rawlins 'a most honest man'. Both may well have been fellow Independents, which would go a long way to explaining the regiments behaviour during the unsettled period after the first Civil War.

Pye's regiment formed part of the horse commanded by Colonel Vermuyden which were sent north in May 1645. They were to give assistance to the Scottish army. On reaching Leicester, Pye was asked to stay and assist the town with its defences. The town was ill-prepared for the ruthless storming undertaken by Prince Rupert on 30 May. A three hour bombardment tore a gaping hole in the walls and while men and women tried to repair the breach Pye and major Innes led a defence that repulsed a number of assaults. When the Royalist's, finally broke in it took a house to house fight before the Roundheads capitulated. Their frustration over the determination of the defenders led to some of the worst excesses of the war. Little quarter was given and the town, was looted. Pye was made prisoner but parolled on 4 June. (8) His parole did not allow him to take part in the battle of Naseby, but his regiment, was there in full strength, on the right wing under Cromwell.

In September 1645 Pye's regiment was part of the force which successfully lay siege to Bristol and the following May Pye was detached to secure his own home Faringdon House. (9)

With the first Civil War over, Parliament was faced with the problem of a large Scottish army still in England. It was decided to pay them off and Pye's troops made up part of the escort conveying the money north in January 1647. When the money was paid the Scots handed over the King and it was Pye's regiment that escorted him to Holdenby House. Once there they formed part of the guard.

Parliament, divided between Presbyterians and Independents, with the majority in the Presbyterian camp, now had the thousands of soldiers in the New Model to deal with. It was clumsily proposed to disband half the army while the remainder would either assist in policing England or volunteer for service in Ireland.

Pye urged his men to accept service in Ireland but there was a great deal of argument and his troopers wrote to the agents of the regiments of horse who were with the main army at Saffron Walden. The agents were petitioning against disbanding and Pye's men expressed agreement with their aims. When Pye attempted to change their minds he was surrounded by mutinous troopers. He was forced to draw his sword but when one of his captains was pulled down from his horse, Pye withdrew for fear of bloodshed. (10) Pye's troopers were typical of the majority. They had not been paid, they faced an insecure future, many demanded liberty of conscience and there was a growing political awareness. The soldiers of the war now wanted a say in the future of the country.

These divisions amongst his enemies brough fresh hope to the King. When the House of Lords elected to invite the King to take up residence at his palace of Oatlands, it was nearer to London for negotiations, the Independents acted.

Cornet Joyce, with 500 mounted men, moved to Oxford to secure the artillery train. From Oxford they rode to Holdenby and siezed the King. With the exception of Major Tomlinson, Pye's regiment made no effort to stop Joyce. The majority of troopers decided to join Fairfax and the main army. Pye, witnessing the emergence of the Independents against the Presbyterians at close quarters, managed to bring his own troop down to London.

Cromwell had already left the capital for fear of being arrested.

When Pye arrived he found he was in company with Major-General Browne in opposing the extremists. Pye quartered at Highgate and Islington. In August, when Fairfax led the army on London, Pye was sent to Deptford. The army encircled London and Major Disbrowe with his men fell upon Pye and his troopers during a parley. Calling them 'runaway rogues', Disbrowe's men killed four of Pye's troopers and wounded several others. Pye was placed under arrest, the Presbyterian attempt to defend London had completely failed, the only bloodshed being at Deptford. Fairfax intervened and Pye was released and he was thanked in Parliament by the Presbyterians for his fidelity. Even so, with others he was compelled to ask for a pass to go beyond the seas, for his own safety.

Robert Pye later came to terms with Cromwell's government. He sat in Parliament in 1654 and 1658 as a member for Berkshire. Going in opposition once again he was sent to the Tower. Released after several months he again represented the county in 1660.

In December 1688 he joined William of Orange on his march to London. Taking no further part in politics, Robert Pye died in 1701.

CHAPTER TWENTYONE

READING - JULY 1647

'Gentlemen, yee may now sit downe and play,
for you have done all your worke,
if you fall not out among yourselves'.
Sir Jacob Astley.

The by-elections of 1645-6 led to an increase in the number of Independents at Westminster. The Presbyterians still had the majority but their opposition had the backing of the New Model Army. The country's problems were not only political; the first peace-time harvest of 1646 failed completely and plague broke out in London, the worst epidemic for ten years. The King, bargaining with his Scottish captors, viewed the increasing divisions with optimism.

In 1647, the influence of the Levellers, led to the army regiments electing agents to represent them and their grievances. Known as 'Agitators' there were two for each regiment, the horse regiments being far more politically minded than the foot. The army had not been paid, they were against Irish service and they wanted freedom of conscience. Most revolutionary of all, they wanted the right to vote. Leveller pamphlets rightly pointed out that they were not mercenaries, but 'called forth and conjured' by Parliament. A Parliament for which the vast majority had no right of voting for, the criteria then being ownership of property. Cromwell supported most of their demands, particularly when it came to freedom of worship (provided it excluded Catholics), but male suffrage was too radical, even for him.

Whole regiments mutinied when the commissioners appointed to disband the army started their work. Colonel Rainsborough's were stationed at Portsmouth awaiting embarkation to Jersey. On 28 May, news reached London that they had mutinied and were marching on Oxford. They were intending to sieze the Train of Artillery, under threat of siezure by Parliament. Rainsborough was sent from London and he met his regiment at Abingdon and it

146

was only with difficulty that he managed to pursuade them from their enterprise. (1) Such interference by high ranking officers led the Levellers pamphleteers to call them 'The Grandees'.

When the House of Lords extended their invitation to the King to come to Oatlands, Cromwell saw danger to himself by remaining in London. Either he or the agitators planned the securing of the King from Holdenby House. The army had mustered at Newmarket and it was there the King and Cromwell met for the first time.

That month the army formed its 'Army Council' and published its Declaration. It stated it had the right to defend its interests and called for Parliament to be dissolved. It was now in Cromwell and the army that the King saw fresh hope for his future.

With the King in their hands, the army marched south intending to protect its interests in London. In July they arrived at Reading where on 16 and 17 July the Council of the Army met. (2) The King was lodged at Lord Craven's house in Caversham. The King was allowed to go, under escort, to Maidenhead. Five shillings was paid to the ringers to herald his coming and the streets were decked with flowers and green boughs. At the Greyhound Inn the King was reunited with his children. Fairfax then allowed the children to accompany their father back to Caversham where they stayed together while the Army Council met. (3)

Presided over by Fairfax, the majority of the council were in favour of marching on London. Cromwell and Ireton argued against the use of force but were over-ruled when Parliament was attacked by the London mob and the Presbyterians went into a war-like defence. The Independents were forced to leave the capital, they could only turn to the army for support. On 6 August, Fairfax led the New Model Army into London and the Presbyterian leaders fled abroad.

The King was lodged at Hampton Court where he was often visited by army leaders. In November debates were hold at Putney in a riverside church and the Levellers, representing

147

London in the mid seventeenth century as seen from the river.

the mass of the army, argued their case. Once again manhood suffrage was the principle talking point which was opposed by the army grandees. Lilburne, the guiding light of the Leveller movement, protested against the law which called for a man to hold 40s worth of property before he had the right to vote.

One parallel he drew was, 'there is a tanner in Staines worth £3000, and another in Reading worth three horseskins'. The Reading tanner had the vote by right of property, the Staines man (4) had none. When the debates broke down and the agitators were ordered to return to their regiments, the King, now in secret negotiation with the Scots, escaped.

WINDSOR - 1647-49

'whether with his enemies or friends, in the Court
or Camp, he was always in the hands of another;
now of his Wife, then of the Bishops; now of the
Peers, then of the Soldiery; and lastly of his enemies.'
John Milton, writing of Charles I.

The King's flight from Hampton Court sealed his fate with the army. Already apprehensive over dealings between the King and the Grandees, the rank and file became vocal in demanding the King be brought to trial.

The King's escape took him to the Isle of Wight. There he hoped for a springboard to the continent and a refuge where he could deal more secretly with the Scots. He placed himself in the hands of the governor of Carisbrooke Castle, Colonel Robert Hammond. Hammond had fought during the war as a captain and he had been at both Newbury battles. Although yet another of Cromwell's relatives, he changed his attitude towards the general as Cromwells policies towards the King had hardened. Hammond still made it his first priority to inform his kinsman and to secure his 'guest'.

During December 1647, a mutiny broke out in the regiments at Ware, inspired by the Levellers. Fairfax and Cromwell, swiftly and ruthlessly, suppressed the outbreak, making a number of arrests and having one man shot at the head of the regiment. The Army Council structure was disbanded and replaced with a Council of Officers.

On December 21 the General Council met at Windsor. A number of courts martial were held in the castle. Mutineers from Ware were tried and a few were sentenced to run the gauntlet through lines of soldiers drawn out into the ward. The main purpose of the meeting was for the members of the army to mend their differences and to present a united front in their effort to dominate the political future of the country.

Cromwell even managed to become reconciled with the Leveller officers. A solemn fast day was held on 22 December and it was spent in earnest prayer, 'They prayed fervently and pathetically, this continued from nine in the morning to seven at night'.(1) Ominously one suggestion that found ready assent at the conference was that the King should be tried as a 'criminal'. The whole council dined with Fairfax at Windsor on 4 January; openly now Charles was being referred to as 'that man of blood'. The last meeting was held on 8 January 1648. 'This Saturday the General Council of the Army met at the Castle at Windsor, and they were very unanimous in debate'. They agreed there should be no further address to the King and promised to support Parliament in settling the affairs of the Kingdom without him. (2)

Within three months the council were back at Windsor. A three day fast and prayer session was followed by a united condemnation of the previous Autumn's negotiations with the King. Unanimously they passed a resolution to bring the King to trial. While the council were sitting, events took a turn which would lead the King to the scaffold; the Second Civil War broke out.

Berkshire was spared a repeat of the horrors of the first war in the uprising of 1648. The main concern that summer for the county was yet another terrible harvest. The floods and resulting damage brought in the highest food prices for a century. The cloth industry had still not recovered and once again starvation became a fact of life in both towns and villages.

The Second Civil War was fought with far more acrimony, Fairfax and Cromwell set about putting the uprising down in a thoroughly ruthless fashion. Berkshire was considered secure enough to warrant one troop of horse to garrison Windsor Castle. The troop was commanded by Colonel Tomlinson who had succeeded Pye as colonel to the regiment.

No sooner had Cromwell brought the Second Civil War to a

conclusion with a stunning victory at Preston, then Parliament repealed the Vote of No Addresses, and were sending negotiators to the King at Newport. Such a move was certain to bring fury to the army grandees and it sent Henry Marten back into Berkshire to start his own little war against Parliament.

Marten, perhaps one of the staunchest anti-Royalists, (then and now), began recruiting his army to oppose Parliament. 'Whereas by virtue of that right which I was born to as an Englishman, and in pursuance of that duty which I owe my said Country, I have resolved to raise and conduct a Regiment of Harquebusiers on horse back on the behalf of the people of England, for the recovery of their freedom', so he wrote to Simon Rice. (3) Raiding stables and holding up travellers in Berkshire, Marten collected his mounts.

'Mercurius Pragmaticus' of 22-29 August took him a little less seriously. Calling him 'Saint Harry' they reported him as being 'in extreme anger that the Houses should presume, contrary to his liking, to proceed so farre as they have done in order to a treaty, for which cause he is resolved to declare against them, in as high terms as ever he did against the King'. Having recruited some horse by swashbuckling methods, he set about raising a regiment of foot, 'the rusticks of Berkshire resorting to him in great numbers'. According to Lilburne, Marten also told the Berkshire jurymen that they were greater men than the judges and therefore should sit with their hats on at assizes. Parliament sent Major Fincher into Berkshire to suppress the uprising and Henry Marten, still unrepentant, returned to his seat in Parliament.

The Commissioners continued their negotiations with the King at Newport. Despite repeated failures, political manoeuvre and intrigue were the King's sole remaining weapons. Throughout the war he never wavered from his first principles which had led to his present unhappy position. To him the Royal Prerogative was inviolate, entrusted to him by God. The control and destiny of his Kingdom and the care of his Subjects were his alone by Divine Right. With that right came the duty to defend it no matter

The execution of King Charles.

what the cost. Charles Stuart, in the rapidly changing 17th century, was made to be a martyr.

Oliver Cromwell had emerged from the Second Civil War as the most successful general of the army. Fairfax, although supreme commander through him all the army demands had to pass, was lost in politics. Behind Cromwell lay some of the cleverest political minds in the army, not least his relative by marriage, Henry Ireton.

During October 1648, Ireton remained at Windsor Castle, charged with drawing up the Army's Remonstrance against the King. Passed to Fairfax, it was forwarded to London for Parliament. It demanded. among other things, that the King, 'the grand author of our troubles', be brought to trial. Even as the Remonstrance was being carried to London, soldiers were on their way to the Isle of Wight to remove Hammond from his position in charge of the King. Hammond, brought back to Windsor Castle, was placed temporarily under arrest.

Parliament, still with a Presbyterian majority, saw England as a Monarchy but Republicanism was in the air. Almost burying their heads in the sand, the House ignored Ireton's manifesto and continued their negotiations with the King.

From petitions presented at Windsor, some may well have been instigated, the army judged it had the country on its side. In November, 'divers of the Committee, Gentry, Ministry, and other well-affected of the county of Berks'; 'presented His Excellency with their 'humble petition'. Fairfax backed it and sent it on to London, thus demonstrating the 'countrys' attitude reflected that of the army. The petition bears all the marks of having been framed by Ireton and other army grandees.

The petitioners 'Desir'd Execution of Justice upon all great offenders' an obvious reference to the King. Filled with cant the petition declared that without such punishments there could be 'no exercise of Religion, no use of Lawes, no Assurance of Libertie or Protection'. It continues, 'all the world shall see it was in your

153

Hearts only to serve the necessity of the Nation,

During the hours of darkness, on 30 November, troops from Windsor crossed over to the Isle of Wight. His attendants, alarmed by the approach of 40 horse and 200 foot, urged the King to escape. One courtier even demonstrated how easily it could be done by walking past the guards and back in again wearing a soldiers cloak. Stubbornly the King refused, maintaining he had given his word to Parliament. It was unceremoniously pointed out to him that the musketeers surrounding the house at this moment, their matches smoking in the damp night air, were not Parliament, but the dreaded army. The King retired to bed, convince they had come to murder him. The following morning, with very little courtesy, he was transferred to the mainland and locked up in Hurst Castle.

Notified that the soldiers had achieved their aim, the Army Council ordered another march on London. As the capital rang with the tramp of marching feet, Parliament fruitlessly debated the Newport Treaty and condemned the unauthorised removal of the King from the Isle of Wight.

During the night of 5 December, Ireton placed two regiments around the Palace of Westminster. As a hollow gesture he reported their dispositions to Fairfax. The following morning, as the members arrived, they discovered Colonel Pride on the steps. A list of names in his hands and a repulsive individual by his side to identify members, members were allowed in one by one after vetting.

Those that were stopped from entering were led away and locked in a chamber known as 'hell', soon the room was full. One of these was Sir Benjamin Rudyerd of West Woodhay, brother-in-law to Speaker Lenthall. Rudyerd had been vocal from the beginning with warnings of the horrors of Civil War. Highly regarded in Parliament, he was disgusted with the actions of the Independents and a leading advocate for accommodation with the King. Although 76 years of age he was bundled into 'hell' with the others.

The day following 'Pride's Purge' Cromwell entered London. It was significant that he made his first entrance to the Chamber arm-in-arm with Henry Marten, the totally committed Republican.

The Army Council now decided to remove the King from Hurst to the greater security of Windsor Castle. Colonel Harrison was sent to organise the journey and ensure the security aspects of the passage. Arriving at Hurst Castle he detailed the route to be followed. On being informed of Harrison's arrival the King felt certain that if any, this was the man to kill him. Harrison had been the first to use the term, 'this Man of Blood'. The details completed Harrison left again without meeting his charge. When told he would be moved to Windsor the King remarked, 'leaving the worst for the best castle in England'. Later, on the road, the King and Harrison met for the first time. On seeing the Puritan, well known for his flamboyant mode of dress, the King altered his opinion, being impressed by Harrison's soldier-like appearance.

At Bagshot a poorly planned escape attempt was organised, it was quickly discovered by Harrison. Fearing an armed attempt might be undertaken within the close confines of the Great Park, Harrison sent for reinforcements from Windsor before he would continue.

The townspeople of Windsor lined the streets, standing in cold, wet sleet, to see the King pass. Cries of 'God Bless Your Majesty' were heard, and 'send you long to reign'. Speculation was high, fed by pamphlets which could be bought in every street. When the cavalcade had passed many retired to the local inns to discuss the momentous affairs taking place in the castle. It was not long before fighting broke out and eventually musketeers had to be sent down from the castle to restore order.

Colonel Whichcote, Governor of the Castle, greeted the King as he entered the gates. The eyes of the prisoners, many captured during the recent fighting, followed the slight Royal figure. They had all either fought for him or were sympathetic to his cause, many had probably never seen him before. One distinguished captive, the Duke of Hamilton, once the King's

155

Master of Horse, knelt in the mud to offer homage. Whichcote allowed him to kiss the King's hand. Tears in his eyes he said, 'My dear Master', the guards rudely brushed them apart.

The King was given his usual bedchamber, close to the end of the castle ward. Once installed he was treated with respect and deference, it was not to last. On 22 December Cromwell and Ireton jointly signed a letter of instruction to Governor Whichcote. They had ordered Captain Brayfield of Hewson's regiment with his own and two other companies of foot into Windsor as extra guards. Colonel Harrison was to quarter three or four troops of horse in the vicinity of the castle.

Whichcote was told to place 'within the upper Castle' one troop of horse, 'and that at least one company of Foote att all times bee upon guard there, and that the Bridge betwixt the Castles (if you think fitt bee drawn uppe in the night', The letter went on, 'Alsoe, that noe other prisoners bee lodged in that parte of the Castle'. Hamilton was to be lodged in the Winchester Tower, well away from the King. The two army officers added, 'It is thought convenient that you turne out of the Castle all malignants or Cavalerish inhabitants, (except the prisoners), and as many others of loose and idle persons as you can well ridde out... '. (5)

As the tide of events swept the King nearer to a trial for his life, there occurred a strange event that captures the bizarre, almost supernatural religious attitude of the time. The Army Council were now meeting at Whitehall and their detailed planning for the coming trial was allowed to be interrupted for several days by the visit of a Mrs Elizabeth Poole from Abingdon. (6) She had been subject to revelations in which she had seen God's presence within the army. The army had been shown to her in the form of a man while the country was that of a woman and the man could be the only healer of the woman. Closely questioned by members of the Council, she was asked to remain at Whitehall for further interrogation.

Her second interview found her armed with her visions put into writing, her complex religious argument was that the King was the head of the body (of the wife), and may be placed under restraint by the man (the army), but the husband should not

156

remove that head. Anticipating the King's attitude to any court, Rich asked what would be the case if the King remained mute. Mrs Poole replied, 'I understand it nott'. Was she against the trial they asked?. 'Bring him to Triall, that he may be convicted in his conscience, but touch not his person', she said. Ireton asked should any King be spared no matter how awful his crimes, 'bind his hands and hold him fast' she said 'but not bring about his death'.

The Council then deliberated as to the nature of her revelation, had she experienced a vision or been visited by an angel ? On deciding that it must have been a vision and not a visitation of an angel, she was courteously sent back to Abingdon. The Council continued with what Cromwell would later call, 'the great work'.

Christmas Day was the last formal and stately occasion enjoyed by the King. He dined, as was the Stuart custom, seated under a canopy in full view of any that cared to watch. When Harrison reported next to London he was replaced as the King's principle guardian by Colonel Tomlinson. While treating the King with respect, Tomlinson reduced the number of retainers to six. Night and day the King was to be accompanied by soldiers, when at private devotion was to be the only exception. He was allowed to exercise on the terrace overlooking Eton and the river and he was given the companionship of his dogs. His personal retainers were encouraged to spy on him and report to the army officers, when one refused he was promptly replaced.

Plans for the King's trial went ahead under Ireton's direction. Over one hundred Commissioners were selected from the purged members at Westminster, they included the Recorder of Reading. Two judges were appointed to preside over the trial and one, John Bradshaw, obtained a steel-lined hat as ˉa precaution against assassination. He need not have bothered, not one Royalist attempt was made to save the King.

Speculation was high as to the location of the trial. Windsor was a favourite, with the trial one day and execution the next. A Proclamation, signed by Fairfax, was issued on 9 January, any person 'formerly engaged for the King and now in London to depart the City and 10 miles distant, within twentyfour hours'.

The grandees had decided to risk moving the King for trial in London. The King was placed in a coach drawn by six fast horses. All paths inside the castle were lined with musketeers while outside a troop of horse under Barkstead waited for the coach to leave. When it swept out of the gates the troopers took up stations close to either side. They forced spectators to one side, even driving one rider into a ditch.

The trial began in the Painted Chamber at the Palace of Westminster on Saturday, 20 January 1649. The King was carried from Whitehall in a closed sedan chair. Refusing to recognise the legality of the court, the charges were read to him, ending with, 'the said Charles Stuart as a Tyrant, Traitor and Murderer'.

The charade lasted seven days, at the end only sixtyeight commissioners had the nerve to attend to hear their Sovereign sentenced to death. Part of the evidence that condemned him came from witnesses that had seen piles of dead at both battles of Newbury and testified to the King's presence there.

As Bradshaw mouthed the sentence, stating it to be in the name of the people of England, he was interrupted by a cry from the public gallery. A masked woman stood up and shouted 'not half, not a quarter of the people of England'. Hastily the guards went to remove her. When she took away her mask their attitude turned to respect, it was the wife of Sir Thomas Fairfax. Her outburst caused some consternation among the commissioners and a few began to voice doubts as to what they had formerly agreed. A recess had to be called and in an ante-chamber the waverers faced a towering Oliver Cromwell.

Returning to the chamber, Bradshaw continued his address to the court. He ended with the words, ' ... the said Charles Stuart, as a Tyrant, Traitor, Murderer and a Public enemy, shall be put to death, by the severing of his head from his body'. Refused leave to belatedly address his accusers, now standing in assent to the sentence, the King was led away. Colonel Axtell primed his men to cry out, 'Execution, Justice, Execution', to which the King smiled and said, 'For sixpence they will say as much for their own commanders'.

The following day, a Sunday, was given over to prayer. The King requested his dogs should be removed and he spent the day kneeling with Bishop Juxon. Tomlinson was his guardian and he kept his men firmly under control and would allow none of the insults encouraged by other officers.

A messenger from the Prince of Wales was the last courtier the King saw or would allow to see him. The King made a point of commending Tomlinson to the messenger as a civil and considerate man. The King was allowed to see his children, the Princess Elizabeth and the little Duke of Gloucester, on the Monday. Gravely the King charged the little boy that on no account was he to permit them to make him King, that Divine Right lay with his brother Charles, Prince of Wales. Later, when the children had gone, the King requested Tomlinson to be his escort to the scaffold. Tomlinson said he would if allowed and the King gave him a gold toothpick as a thank you.

On Monday, Cromwell and Ireton were still feverishly gathering signatures for the death warrant, a warrant already made out and partially signed before the verdict. By force or agreement they managed to obtain fiftynine signatures, Henry Marten and Daniel Blagrave were two Berkshire men who signed willingly.

The following day, Colonel Tomlinson, hat in hand, complied with the King's request. They crossed St James's Park on a cold frosty morning, the King wearing two shirts and walking quickly. He was afraid of shivering which might be taken for fear. On the scaffold, erected outside the Banqueting Hall in Whitehall, the King discovered the crowd had been positioned so far back so as not to hear his last speech. He turned and addressed it to Tomlinson.

The Duke of Richmond was charged with the funeral arrangements. The cost was not to exceed £500. Over half this sum went on the furnishings for the journey to Windsor. A coach drawn by six black horses carried the body. Black dressed attendants rode in four coaches behind the hearse, two coaches draped in black. Three dozen torches lit the way as the small coffin was borne into the Dean's House which Harrison had had draped yet again in black. Later the body was removed to the King's bedchamber.

The next day, 8 January, Richmond accompanied by Hertford, Lindsay and Southampton, arrived and inspected the Chapel for a suitable place to bury the King. They rejected the site chosen by Whichcote and paid a man 5s 6d to open a vault which contained the remains of Henry VIII and his third wife, Jane Seymour.

On 9 January, 1649 (1648 old date), it snowed very lightly at Windsor. Four soldiers from the garrison carried the Royal coffin from the bedchamber, across the ward, down and into St George's Chapel. The four nobles held the ends of the black pall, now turning white with snow. Under the pall and on the coffin top was a roughly cut piece of lead. Richmond had scratched into its softness:

KING CHARLES   1648.

'and stopping here heard a voice revile
What no more due to such a sacred pile
Can these be his just obsequies
Who least a tongue should suffice
To huzza mighty Charles home
into his martyred fathers roome
Himself hung up a bell to ring
A gladsome entry to the King
Distress nere made him leave King, Church or friend
And growing riches made him grow more kind. '

Inscription to William Phillips
St Mary's Church, Ashbury.

On 29 May, 1660, Charles II entered London, the people rejoiced,
'That the King comes home in peace again',.

Sites to Visit

Berkshire, as a county, probably has more sites that are connected to the civil war than any other county in England. Within the borders of 'Old Berkshire' the entire war was fought in minature. Not only did it see the bloody conflict of major battles but also bore witness to countless scirmishes, sieges and other minor actions. The main problem any potential visitor has is actually identifying these sites. They are not all great houses and castles but rather they are small, out of the way, places like farms and churches. Below we have listed a few sites that are easy to find and can be used as a starting point to discover other places of interest. Happy wanderings.

Abingdon
Once the county town of Berkshire, Abingdon grew prosperous from agriculture and the wool trade. A centre of civil war activity, being fortified by both sides in turn, Abingdon has many fine buildings that survive from the period. Among these is the famous bridge, over 150 yards long that was originally built in the fifteenth century, and was fortified during the civil war. The Borough Museum, housed in the 'County Hall', is of great interest with exhibits ranging from pre-history to the present day. It is here, in the towns archives, that the ten borough charters are kept, the earliest dating from 1556.

Basing house
Although not quite within the borders of Berkshire, Basing House is well worth a visit. Built as a fortified manor in 1530 it stands on the site of a norman castle and an even earlier Anglo-Saxon fortress that is mentioned in the doomsday book. Queen Elizabeth I stayed here twice, her second visit lasted thirteen days and proved so expensive to her host that he had to have part of the house demolished to pay for it. During the civil war Basing House was at the centre of one of the most long drawn out sieges of the entire war. For almost three years it was the centre of Royalist resistance in the area until, in 1645, it was finally captured and

razed to the ground. A museum on site gives an incite into the troubled history of the house and is well worth a visit. The church of St. Mary was also damaged during the civil war but has been restored several times since.

Donnington Castle
Originally built in the late fourteenth century, Donnington castle underwent a long siege during the civil war. Although the twin towered gatehouse is the only major surviving piece of the original castle it is still possible to make out some of the earthworks erected during the siege. Donnington is also probably one of the best vantage points to view the site of the second battle of Newbury as it was fought almost directly below it. Donnington Castle is now in the care of English Heritage.

Newbury
Nestling at the foot of the Berkshire downs, Newbury became prosperous in the middle ages when John Winchcombe (Jack of Newbury) established the first real factory in England here. His cloth factory employed over a thousand people and established Newbury as a centre for the wool trade.

During the civil war the town was in sympathy with the Parliamentry cause and this led to it being the site of two major battles (1643 and 1644). The first battle, a bloody conflict fought among the hedgerows to the southwest of the town, led to the death of Lord Falkland whose monument can still be seen today. The second battle, fought to the north of the town, left both sides believing they had been defeated. Both armies withdrew under cover of darkness. Newbury today boasts a fine museum and has displays dealing with both battles and other topics of local interest.

Oxford
The city of Oxford lies just to the north of the Berkshire county boundary and its position is probably the cause of much of the trouble suffered by Berkshire during the civil war. After the first battle of the war at Edgehill Charles chose Oxford to be his base of operations throughout the war. It was from Oxford that he

sent forth his armies to wage war on the rebels and it was the prize that the Parliamentry commanders most sought.

The city was heavily fortified during the period with earthworks and gun emplacements being erected around the whole of its boundary. The old castle was used as a prison for captive rebels where they were kept in apalling conditions. The town finally fell to General Fairfax in the summer of 1646. The city centre today has changed little in general layout since the time of the civil war. Most of the college buildings were used by the Kings troops in one way or another and many museums, of which the Ashmolean must be considered the finest, contain items that relate to the period.

Windsor
The castle at Windsor played an important part in the civil war, not just in Berkshire, but nationally. It formed a prison, training ground and stronghold for the Parliamentry cause. Although much of the exterior is now ninteenth century the ground plan has changed little in the last 350 years and it is easy to see why it formed such a strategic part of the rebels defences around London.

Windsor town also played an important part in the war. It not only helped supply the castle with both men and materials but also acted as a trade centre for the area. Today Windsor Guildhall has many exhibits that show off this towns proud history and many relate directly to the civil war.

164

NOTES TO THE TEXT

Chapter I
I Songs and Marches of the Roundheads and Cavaliers. L. Winstock. 1971.
2. Calendar of State Papers, Domestic Series. (CSPD) July, 1625.
3. ibid. August, 1630. (A Berkshire case)
4. ibid. December 31st, 1630
5. ibid. August, 1632
6. ibid. January 16th, 1631
7. ibid. December 6th, 1630
8. Dictionary of National Biography. (DNB)
9. CSPD. November 13th, 1633. cf. Rushworth, App. Vol. Ill.
10. CSPD. June 29th, 1627
11. Life of Hampden, App. Lord Nugent. 1831
12. For a modern life of Hampden see, John Hampden the Patriot. John Adair. 1976
13. CSPD. February, 1638
14. ibid. August Ilth, 1638
15. ibid. April, 1639
16. ibid. July, 1640
17. ibid.
18. ibid.
19. ibid. December 13th, 1639
20. ibid. March 26th, 1640
21. Memorials of the English Affairs. Buistrode Whitelock. 1682.
22. The Long Parliament. M. F. Keeler. 1954. cf. Berks. Arch. Jou The Elections of 1640.
23. CSPD. 1640. p. 466. cf - PRO. S. P. 16 Vol. 466,/42. cf. The Revolt in the Provinces. J. S. Morri I I. 1976.
24. For details of Park riots see, CSPD. 1642-3. cf. Annals of Windsor. Vol II. Tighe and Davis. cf. The English People and the English Revolution. B. Manning. 1976.
25. Annals of Windsor. Tighe and Davis. 1858.
26. ibid.
27. Thomason Tracts. British Museum. (TT) E. 69. f. 4(75)

Chapter II.
1.CSPD. September 22nd. 1627.
2. ibid. April, 1639.
3. ibid. July, 1640. Notes made by Sir Edmund Sawyer in regard to the pressing of soldiers.
4. CSPD. June 18th to June 23rd. 1640. cf. Historical Collections of Private Passages of State etc; John Rushworth. 1-659-1701.
5. Cromwell's Army. C. H. Firth. University Paperback. 1967.
6. CSPD. August 10th, 1626.
7. Oliver Cromwell's Letters and Speeches. Thomas

Carlyle. 1897.
8. Sir Samuel Luke's Diary of the Siege of Reading. leth April, 1643; Coates, History of Reading. 1802.
9. TT. E. 22 (I 0)
10. CSPD. August 1628.
11. Sergeant Foster's account, see Chapter Six.
12. Military Memoir of Colonel John Birch. Camden Soc. 1873.
13. Cheriton 1644. John Adair. 1973. cf. The Court Martial Papers of Sir William Waller's Army. J. Adair. Jour. Soc. Army Hist. Res. Vol. 46.

Chapter III
1. DNB. cf. Henry Marten and the Long Parliament. 1. Waters. 1973.
2. TT. El 26 (42) cf. Memoirs of Prince Rupert and the Cavaliers. B.E.G. Warburton. 1849.
3. Parish Registers.
4. The Quarters of the Army thus settled the ninth of December 1642 at Oxford. BM. Harl. MS. 6851. Reprinted in Edgehill; P. Young. 1967.
5. Parish Registers.
6. The Life and Letters of Sir Lewis Dyve. Ed. H. G. Tibbutt. Bed. Hist. Rec. Soc. 27. 1948.
7. Journal of Sir Samuel Luke. Ed. 1. G. Phillip. Oxon. Rec. Soc. 1950-53.
8. ibid.
9. P.R. 0. W. 0. 55/4E-'J. Reprinted in Edgehill; Young.
10. DNB.
11. Prince Rupert. Warburton.
12. The Late Famous Victory obtained by Captain Lanley. Tract in Reading Reference Library.
13. TT. E81. (1)
14. TT. E85. (6)
15. E85 (30)
16. The Civil War in Hampshire. G. N. Godwin. New Edition. 1973.
17. Acts and Ordinances of the Interegnum. C. H. Firth and R. S. Raite 191 I. cf. The Berks Bucks and Oxon Committees. Berks. Arch. Jour. 1 927-29.
18. CSPD. October, 1643. Reprinted in the First and Second Battles of Newbury. W. Money. 2nd Edition. 1864.

Chapter IV
1. The History and Antiquities of Berkshire. Elias Ashmole. 1719.
2. A Brief Chronicle of the Late Intestine Warr. J. Heath. 1663.
3. TT. El26. (42) and E242. (21).
4. DNB.
5. DNB. cf. Cromwell Is Generals. M.P. Ashley. 1954.
6. Annals of Windsor; Tighe and Davis.
7. CSPD.
8. Hist and Ant. of Berks; Ashmole. cf. The Court at Windsor. C. Hibbert.
9. Annals of Windsor; Tighe and Davis. Victoria County History of Berks. (VCH) A List of Names of the Capital Prisoners sent to Windsor Cast I e the 1

1 th January 1642. (1643). Royalist Prisoners in Windsor Castle. Sir Owen Morshead. Berks. Arch. Jour. 56. 1958.

Chapter V
1. Tracts in Reading Reference Library.
2. ibid.
3. Lords Journals. Vi. 17.
4. Another Happy Victory... Tract in Reading Ref. Lib.
5. King Charles I's Army in 1642. P. Young. Jour. Soc. Army. Hist. Res. 17. 1938.
Other Sources.
Siege Diary./Jour. Sam Luke. TT. E92.(2) E99. (16) EIOO. (I 1) El 12. (3) El 26. (43). El 29. (12). Numerous tracts in Reading Ref. Lib. Military Memoirs. John Gwynne.

Chapter VI
1. Mercurius Aulicus. 26th, 28th, August 1643.
2. TT. E69. (15)
3. TT. E69. (1 5)
4. TT. E69. (9)
5. Byron's Account of the Battle. TT. E69. E70.
Other Sources.
First and Second Battles of Newbury. Money. The English Civil War. P. Young and R. Holmes. 1974. Battles and Generals of the Civil Wars. H. C. B. Rogers. 1968. History of the Rebellion. Edward Earl of Clarendon. Oxford 1826. History of the Rebellion. J. Hooper. 1738. TT. E70 (I 0) E6 9 (1 0) El 4 (16) Sergeant Foster's Account is reprinted in History of the Honourable Artillery Company. G.A. Raikes. 1878/9. Battles in Britain. Vol. 2. W. Seymour. 1975. Hurt Soldiers of Newbury. BM. Harl.MSS. 6804. f 92. Reprinted in Jour. Army Hist. Res. 18. P. Young.

Chapter VII
1. Historical Collections; Rushworth.
2. Lords Jours. Vol VI. p. 505.
3. Hist. Coll; Rushworth.
4. Diary of the Marches of the Royal Army. R. Symonds. Edited C. E. Long. Camden Soc. 1859.
5. Civil War in Hants; Godwin.
6. CSRD.
7. Historical Discourses. Sir Edward Walker. 1705.
8. Hist. Coll. ; Rushworth.
9. Mercurius Aulicus 2nd June.
Other Sources.
Exact Dyarie of the progresse of Sir William Waller's Army Richard Coe. 1644. TT F-2. (20). Cropredy Bridge. 1644. M. Toynbee and P. Young. 1970. Roundhead General. J. Adair. 1969. Abingdon Parish Registers. See also. The Church and Parish of St Nicholas, Abingdon. A. E. Preston. 1929. Muster Roll of Reading Garrison. BM. Harl. MSS. 986. Reprinted in Jour. Hist. Army Res. 18. P. Young.

Chapter VIII
1. DNB. cf. Cheriton. J. Adair. 1973.
2. Hist. Col 1. ; Rushworth.
3. The Berks. Bucks and Oxon Committees. Berks. Arch. Jour. 31-3. 1927-9.
4. Battles of Newbury; W. Money.
5. Portland MSS. 13th App. Part 1.
6. CSPD. 1644.
7. ibid.
8. ibid.

Chapter IX
Sources.
Dictionary of National Biography.
Lives of Sir Henry Gage; Sir John Smith. 1645.
CSPD. 1644.
Love Loyalty; Wilf Emberton. 1972.
Civil War in Hants; Godwin.
Clarendon.

Chapter X
Sources.
The Civil War, Young and Holmes.
The Civil War. M. Ashley. 1974. The King's War. C. V. Wedgwood. 1958.
Clarendon.
Civil War in Hants; Godwin.
Lives and Letters of the Devereux, Earls of Essex.. W. B. Devereux. 1853.
Battles of Newbury; Money.

Chapter XI
Sources.
Battle of Newbury; Money.
Diary; Symonds.
Prince Rupert. . ; Warburton.
English Civil War- Young and Holmes.
TT El 4. (16)
Clarendon. Cromwell,
Our Chief of Men; Antonia Fraser. 1973.
Mercurius Aulicus.
Memoirs; Gwynne.
Charles I Is Army. P. Young. Jour. Soc. Army Hist. Res. 18. 1939.
A True Relation. Simeon Ashe. TT. E22 (1 0).
King's War; Wedgwood.

Chapter XII
Sources.
Battles of Newbury; W. Money.
Donnington Castle. H. M.S. Pub. Reprint. 1969.
CSPD.
Symond's Diary.

Chapter XIII
I - CSPD. Sources.
Diary; Symond's.
Prince Rupert; Warburton.
TT E903. (3).
Battles of Newbury; Money.

Chapter XIV
Sources.
The Lord Digbies Designe to Betray Abingdon. TT. E268 (7)
Rushworth.
CSRD. 1644-5.
A Full Relation. Col. Sam. Harsnet. Jan. 12 1644.
A Full Relation of the Victory. . TT. E325 (23).

Chapter XV
1 Tanner MSS. Bodl. Lib. Vol. 60-2. No. 491.
2. The Regimental History of Cromwell's Army. Sir C. H. Firth. 1940.

Chapter XVI
1 . CSPD. 1644-5.
2. Letters and Speeches; Carlyle.
3. Anglia Rediviva; Joshua Sprigge. 1647.
4. CSPD. July 15th, 1645.
Sources.
Historical Discourses... ; Walker.
Diary; Symonds.
Clarendon.
Mercurius Aulicus. May Sth-9th. 1645.
Prince Rupert. . ; Warburton.
History of the Great Civil War; S. R. Gardiner. 1886-91.
Faringdon in the Civil War. C. H. Hartmann. 1966.

Chapter XVII
1.TT. E293 (9).
2. Portland MS. H. M. C. 13th Report. App. Part 1. p. 246/7. 1891.
Sources.
The Clubman of the English Civil War. 0. Warner. Army
Quarterly. 38. 1939.
Civil War in Hants; Godwin.
The Revolt in the Provinces; Morill.

Chapter XVIII
1. Perfect Occurrences of Both Houses of Parliament.
Sources.
News from Dennington Castle. TT. E330. (13).
These and other references to the Donnington Siege are
reprinted in Battles of Newbury; Money.

169

CSPD.

Chapter XIX
I . CSPD.
2. TT. E325.,(23)
3. TT. E330. (21)
4. The Siege of Oxford; F. J. Varley. 1932.
5. Military Memoirs of the Great Civil War. J. Gwyn. Ed. Sir Walter Scott. 1822.
New Edition. Ed. P. Young and N. Tucker. Longmans. 1967.
I place Gwyn's description of events at this date as he states the governor of
Faringdon to be Sir William Courtney. Lisle and Burges commanded
Faringdon and both were at Oxford during the final days, Courtney must
therefore have taken command during the siege.

6. T T. E 3 41. (6)
7 . T T. E341. (1 5) (9).
8 . TT. E345. (19)
9. Anglia Rediviva; Sprigge.
Sources.
Faringdon in the Civil War; Hartmann.

Chapter XX
1 . D. N. B. For details of the regiment's history see, Regimental History; Firth.
2. CSPD. September 12th, 1642.
3. Life and Times of Anthony Wood. Ed. A. Clark. 1891.
4. Prince Rupert's Diary - Wilts. Record Office. Reprinted in Edgehill; P. Young.
5. Studies and Illustrations of the Great Rebellion; Sandford.
6. Journal; Sir Sam. Luke.
7. Diary; Symonds.
8. Leicester During the Civil War; Hollings. 1 840.
9. Anglia Rediviva; Sprigge.
10. Lords Jour. IX. p. 21 4. cf. Clarke Papers. Vol. p. 113.
11. Hist. Coll. - ; Rushworth.
12. Memoirs; Whitelock.

Chapter XXI
1 . Clarke Papers. Vol. 1. p. 176.
2. Hist. of the Great Civil War; Gardiner.
3. TT. E398. (2)
4. Puritanism and Liberty: the Army Debates. A. S. P. Woodhouse. 1

Chapter XXII
1 Clarke Papers. cf. Perfect Diurnal Wed. Dec. 22. 1647.
2. Rushworth.
3. Clarke Papers. cf. CSPD.
4. A True Copie of the Berkshire Petition. TT. E475. (2) cf. Victoria County
History of Berks.
5. Clarke Papers. Col. 2. p. 1 42.
6. TT. E537. (24). E555. (23,24). cf. Clarke Papers. Vol. 2.

Sources.
The Trial of Charles 1. C. V. Wedgwood. 1964.
The Trial of Charles the First; A Contemporary Account taken from the memoirs of Sir Thomas Herbert and John Rushworth; Ed: Roger Lockyer. Folio Press. 1974.
Cromwell. . ; Antonia Fraser.
Charles the First; John Bowie. 1975.

Picture Credits

The publishers would like to express their sincere gratitude to Greenhill Books, a division of Lionel Leventhal Ltd, for their kind permission to reproduce images from their edition of 'The Exercise of Arms' by Jacob De Gheyn. Thankyou.
The publishers would also like to thank the following for their kind permission to reproduce images used in this publication.

Front Cover - Main picture G.A.Embleton
                          Background courtesy of The National Trust.

Chapter tailpieces taken from a coin of Charles the first (G.A.E)

Private collection G.A.E   (chapters 1,7,15,19,21)
Ashmolean Museum, Oxford   (chapters 2,3,9,11,22)
Greenhill Books   (chapter 17)
ADC Pictures   (chapter 4,13,18)
The Devonshire Collection, Chatsworth House.   (chapter 6)
Reproduced by permission of the Chatsworth Settlement Trustees:
Photograph - Courtauld Institute of Art